Letting Go
of
Baggage

A Journey through Life's Challenges

Peter M. Kalellis

PAULIST PRESS
New York/Mahwah, NJ

Cover design by Trudi Gershenov
Book design by Lynn Else

Library of Congress Cataloging-in-Publication Data

Kalellis, Peter M.
    Letting go of baggage : a journey through life's challenges / Peter M. Kalellis.
      p. cm.
    ISBN 978-0-8091-4494-5 (alk. paper)
    1. Christian life. 2. Memory—Religious aspects—Christianity. 3. Regret—Religious aspects—Christianity. 4. Forgiveness—Religious aspects—Christianity. 5. Conscience—Religious aspects—Christianity. 6. Peace of mind—Religious aspects—Christianity. I. Title.
    BV4509.5.K3155 2007
    248.4—dc22

2007027453

Published by Paulist Press
997 Macarthur Boulevard
Mahwah, New Jersey 07430

www.paulistpress.com

Printed and bound in the
United States of America

This book is dedicated with
affection and love to the newlyweds,
my daughter Katina and her husband Peter,
with all good wishes for a long and happy life.

Contents

Acknowledgments

I am grateful to

...my beloved, magnificent wife of thirty years. She has stood by me as I struggled to cope with life's transitions, and as I obsessed over writing psychospiritual self-help books. I am a lucky man, and I love her dearly.

...my four loving and nurturing children—Mercene, Mike, Basil, and Katina—who encourage me to continue writing.

...my dear friend and wise mentor, Wendell Shackelford, who reads my manuscripts and suggests improvements.

...my coworker Margery Hueston, who gave the original draft shape and form.

...my friend Patti Manzi, who diligently edited the final draft.

...the staff of Paulist Press for comments and suggestions to make this effort worthwhile.

...my colleagues, who appreciate my work and periodically invite me to their communities to conduct weekend seminars.

...and to the managing editor of Paulist Press, Paul McMahon, who encouraged my writing, fired my zeal at every step, and kept me enthusiastic, coherent, and structured.

Introduction

In 1925, abandoning the deprivation of a village in a Greek island, my parents emigrated from their native land and sailed to America, the promised land of wealth and opportunity. Within two years, on June 3, 1926, my parents brought me into the world in the City of Brotherly Love, Philadelphia. Seventy-seven years have passed since the Creator placed me in the arms of affection, replete with reality and life's complexities. Yet, I have still not learned some of the basic secrets of life, nor do I comprehend fully the mysteries of love or hate, birth or death, the concept of truth or justice or greed, and the cruel reality of war.

Several wars have taken place during my lifetime, yet I look forward to the end of the current conflicts and the rebuilding of a world at peace. At the dawn of peace following World War II, a cold war broke out, and when that uneasy situation was eventually settled, we became involved in another war. It is said that history repeats itself, and where wars are concerned, that seems to be the case. Warmongers conspire to destroy what appears to be peaceful times: on Tuesday, September 11, 2001, the United States was viciously attacked by terrorists, challenging our cherished ideals of freedom, safety, and peace. America, which for so long had enjoyed a period of unprecedented peace and prosperity, was invaded by an enemy. The American dream of superpower, material wealth, and security was shattered. Our nation suffered a horrendous loss of three thousand people, leaving peace-loving citizens in deep grief and in constant fear of another terrorist attack.

Questions often arise: *With all the accomplished, brilliant, and inventive minds of our times, why is it that we cannot build bridges of understanding through diplomacy, and cultural and commercial exchange? Why can't the leaders of each nation learn to cooperate with one another to achieve mutual peace and wellness? With all the sophisti-*

cated means of communication available, why is it that we cannot develop cooperation and encourage trust? The more governments learn to accept and trust one another, the less will nations succumb to fear, aggression, and war.

During my life, I have traveled extensively with family, friends, compatriots, and foreigners, and I have witnessed many wonders of the world. Even now my mind still envisions fantasies of new places where I might find peace, experience more pleasure, and attain more knowledge. My soul is still restless, yearning to know answers to questions that haunt me: *What is my purpose in life? What is truth? What is the real truth about me? Who is God and what is his ultimate plan for the world?*

Every seven years of my life, something significant has happened. Studies in biology claim that every seven years all the cells of our body are renewed. We see and feel the physical changes, the different forms we go through, as we grow. It is beyond my comprehension how this happens, yet every seven years, my emotional, physical, and mental lives have gone through major changes. In my search for a better life in a better country, the promised land, I have progressed through many transitions.

On my seventy-seventh birthday, after the pleasant amenities of an elegant party, I withdrew from the celebration and settled myself in my study to relax, meditate, and ponder. *Where did the years go?* I closed my eyes and let my mind, the fastest vehicle in the world, take me back in time.

Events unfolded and became sharp and clear as if they had occurred yesterday. Each episode flashed through my mind, impacted my spirit, retreated swiftly, and vanished. Between feelings of happiness and sadness, I grappled with what seemed to be important moments, outstanding personalities, and experiences that had shaped my character and made me who I am today. I held on to each event separately and tried to relive it. I saw people, places, and things, treasured objects in a forgotten closet, with new vision.

In the world around us, the faces of our fellow travelers are sculpted by life's joys and sorrows not unlike our own. If we truly look at our brothers and sisters, we shall see ourselves in the mirror of their eyes. Made as we are in the image and likeness of

God, our hearts cannot rest until they rest in him. The work of a lifetime, generation after generation, is the human journey back to God. Our response to this inner call that seeks the True Beginning and the Perfect End is the most important activity of our human experience. It is a personal journey made in time among fellow travelers, and also a timeless journey made into eternity entirely alone. We are shaped and formed as persons by the choices we make and by the historic times in which we live; we are carved by social pressures, personal perceptions, and inner forces. Life is to be the great sculptor of the human heart.

In writing this book, I share with you common aspects of life, at times undesirable yet unavoidable. In reading the following pages, you may discover what formed and shaped your own life. In accepting and acknowledging the totality of who you are, your life should become less burdensome and more rewarding. Surely you will see personal characteristics that you wish were not there. However, they are. You may even be haunted by a syndrome of negative feelings—anger, boredom, depression, fear, hostility, insecurity, jealousy, guilt, and greed. Instead of denying them or pretending they are not part of you, accept them as a reality of the human condition.

All humans are imperfect and need to move on and grow beyond the negative aspects of life. When we open our closet of memories, we do not have to pretend our life was perfect or even think that it could be. Our attitude—how we respond to life and how we interact with others—is more important. What a person learns, even from the toughest lessons of life, is the magic of maturity.

My hope is to convey and confirm realities of life as I have perceived them thus far, so the reader may think, feel, and act with more courage, dignity, humor, generosity, love, patience, peace, and self-respect.

PART ONE
Searching

1

Finding the Love Within

From its earliest days, the child had to learn degrees of approach and withdrawal toward everyone around him. He had to learn whom he could touch, in whose arms comfort and warmth could be sought, where distance was the safer course.
—Margaret Mead

On February 7, 1929, my mother died, and on September 7 of the same year, my father, denying the heartbreak of his loss, returned to Greece to look for another wife. The ocean liner *Edison* crossed the Atlantic Ocean in fifteen cold and turbulent days. The sparkling "Diamond of the Aegean," the island of Lesvos, made no impression on my three-year-old mind. How I arrived in a little village there, I have no recollection. Without explanation, my father had moved me from my familiar surroundings in Philadelphia and planted me in his native village of Moria, where I had to adjust to loving yet unknown relatives in a foreign land. For me, it was emotional exile.

"I want a mother for my motherless son," he told his relatives, lest taunting tongues criticize him for wanting to remarry so soon after his wife's death.

Yet he lied to me.

"I want Mommy," I cried in despair.

"Your mother is in a hospital in America. When she gets well, she'll come to us," my father said in a firm voice, trying to comfort me with words he knew to be false.

My inner lamentation turned into sobbing, and tears overflowed in a river down my sad face.

One afternoon, a girl of about nine years of age visited us. She had long hair, rosy cheeks, and skinny legs, and she was holding two kittens in her arms.

"My name is Galatia, and I want you to have these," she said, handing me the tiny kittens.

At the sight of those pearly blue eyes and pink noses, I smiled. My tears stopped flowing. Something magic was happening to me. The kittens were soft, and they had beautiful white fur with symmetrical brown spots on their face and body. They exuded an extraordinary feeling of love. They snuggled in my arms and purred. For that second, I no longer wanted anything or anybody. I had my kittens; they were my whole world and I was their whole world. It was a moment that marked the beginning of my love for cats, which continues to be an irreplaceable source of love in my life.

I still believed my mother was in America, and that some day she would come back to me. Nobody told me she had died. Although the idea of death was beyond my comprehension—an abstract idea too far removed from my three-year-old experience— if someone had tried to explain the situation to me, I am sure I would have eventually gained a little comfort. My only experience had been a life with my mother who had responded to my every need—feeding me, smiling at me, telling me stories, and amusing me with toys. How could she disappear all of a sudden? When was she coming back to see me? Every day upon wakening, I asked the same questions: "Where is Mommy? When is she coming back?" One day I looked at my father with rage and cried, "Let's go back to America now. I don't like it here."

My grandmother was the only one who understood how I felt. I called her *Yiayia*—one of the first Greek words I learned. She was bosomy, grief-stricken, tall, and elegant. A widow, she always dressed in black, and her wrinkled cheeks were framed in a black mantle, a sign of mourning. I saw her as a pillar of power, lifting me up in her arms, pouring affection on me, her eyes glittering with the smile on her face. At bedtime, Yiayia lulled me to sleep; I nestled my head between her mountainous breasts and visualized my mother.

One Sunday after church, instead of taking our familiar path to Yiayia's, my father took me to a house in a different neighborhood. Anxiously he knocked at the door, which was answered by a huge woman. From the kitchen came the smell of cooking.

"Good morning and welcome," the woman said hesitantly, blushing. "Please come in. I have been waiting for you."

Waiting for me? She doesn't even know me! My face turned red, temples thudded, and I looked suspiciously from my father to the woman I was meeting for the first time.

My father leaned forward and kissed her, and with all my strength, I grabbed him by the leg and growled, "Let's go to my Yiaa...yiaa!"

"Peter, this is your mother. She has come from America."

"That's not Mommy," I hissed through my teeth.

Smiling nervously, the stranger bent over me. "Of course I'm your Mommy," she said, simulating a feeling of caring and trying to take me in her arms. "Don't you remember me? I'm well now, and I'm back, and I'll be with you forever. Let me hold you in my arms the way I used to. Let me tell you how much I've missed you." Her words seemed cold and rehearsed.

"No," I said emphatically, and I noticed a grimace of disappointment in her face. Clinging to my father, I stared at her. I knew she was not my mother. She didn't look or smell like my mother. "I want my kittens. Let's go to Yiayia's," I whimpered and wedged my face between my father's knees.

"We'll be just fine here," he said.

"No, it won't be fine," I sobbed. There was sadness in his face. I wanted to hug him and hold him and take his grief and merge it with my own. Yet I also wanted to shake him and accuse him of lying and trying to trick me. But I couldn't talk to him about how I felt and how painful it was not to have my real mother. I wanted my father to be a friend, like the girl who had brought me the kittens, and I felt more pain realizing that he could not be my friend. At a very young age, I reached the conclusion that most adults do not listen to their children. Even when I became older, my father would still not listen to what I had to say.

We did not return to my grandmother's house for many years. I was not allowed to see her at all. Yiayia, like my mother, had disappeared from my life; the kittens had disappeared from my life. I felt literally split in two. I was aware that my grandmother's home, where I had felt majestic, was permeated with love. Now, I had lost that haven. I had to succumb to my father's new environment, live with his new wife, Katerina, and try not to think or feel.

At first Katerina was a loving woman and made efforts to please me. But can anyone satisfy a child who has lost the primary love, his mother? She provided meals, clothes, shelter—evidence of her caring for my physical needs. But as a three-year-old boy I seemed to be caught in a web of my own fantasy: *My real mother exists somewhere else, perhaps far away. Maybe my father didn't like her and left her somewhere. Some day she may return to me miraculously.*

Taken up with the role of mother, Katerina had difficulty in allowing me to become an individual different from herself. Most likely she resented the fact that I was not her own child, and my presence interfered with her newlywed life. In her effort to make my father a happy husband, she made it her mission to try to convince him that she could be a real mother to me.

"You have forgotten me because I had to stay in the hospital for such a long time."

She repeated this line, and in a loving way served it to me at bedtime for several nights. But the only response from me was a sigh and a sad face.

Deep inside I felt loneliness and an inability to say what was in my heart. The words, words of pain and shock in response to lies, failed to come out. My feelings of being denied my real mother's love were stifled and trapped inside me. My words could not adequately convey the incredible impact that this strange environment had upon me. Katerina, soon detached and speechless, towered over my bed and stared at me. She heard only my sigh, not aware that it was my soul crying in the darkness as I slowly came to the realization that I had no mother to truly love me and whom I could love in return.

To take up residence in my stepmother's house was a huge change for me after having lived with my grandmother for a long time. Hoping to gain favors in order to be allowed someday to visit Yiayia, I played along with the big lie and called my father's new wife "Mamma." I wished I could believe that she really was, but Katerina's lack of motherly love was obvious. She forbade me to make friends, and that was particularly stressful for me.

During my first year in elementary school, Katerina gave birth to a little girl, Kiki. A year later, she added a baby boy, Jimmy, to the family. Having to care for my two baby siblings, she had little time to cater to the needs of a six-year-old boy who was grieving and starving for affection.

My feelings of rage and jealousy grew day by day. I was especially disturbed to watch the outpouring of Mamma's affections on her own two children. I was not her son. I knew she would have preferred not to have me around. Feeling ignored and rejected, I wished Kiki and Jimmy would disappear as suddenly as my mother and grandmother and kittens had. *If Katerina wishes to be my mother, she will have to love only me,* I thought. But that was never to be. These two uninvited guests came into my life, and they were there to stay, devouring Katerina's affections and leaving me a loveless little boy yearning for attention. I was a shadow in her life, a shadow that had no feelings, no power, and no love. My heart ached when I saw mothers hugging their children, or when I heard the children calling, "Mama! Mama!" How sweet their voices sounded!

The time came when I was old enough to join a Cub Scout program. Afraid that I might secretly visit Yiayia, Katerina said, "There is no time for cubs." She allowed me to watch the Cub Scouts from our second-floor window as they paraded past our house, dressed in their khaki uniform and blue scarf. Seething with frustration, I held my tears, but in bed I wept inconsolably. How much I wanted to be one of those lucky boys and take part in the parade!

My sister, Kiki, being Katerina's first child, objected to my presence in her life. She wanted Mamma's love totally to herself. When Mamma spoke to me gently or did something good for me, Kiki showed resentment. One evening, as Kiki was being tucked into bed, I overheard Katerina say, "Kiki, you've got to be good to your brother Peter and love him. It isn't his fault that he's motherless. I am your real mother, but he's not like you—he doesn't have a real mother. He's an orphan." The word *orphan* was used by the villagers to denote a child who had lost one parent.

The word *orphan* remained emblazoned on my mind for many, many years. Whenever I heard the word, I shivered. One Sunday afternoon my parents took me to a wedding at St. Basil's Church. During the service, the priest lit a white candle and gave it to me to hold as I stood next to the bridal pair. Nervously excited among the happy attendants, I grew several inches taller instantly, feeling manly and proud. That ray of joyful exuberance was cruelly interrupted by a hand that forced itself through the crowd and snatched my candle away, leaving me in utter shock. The villagers were full of superstitions. It was believed that bad luck would follow a bridal pair whose candle holder was an orphan.

The priest shook his head, placed a compassionate hand on my shoulder, and whispered, "Another silly superstition." It was as if orphanhood was an incurable, contagious disease. I backed away and hid in a corner of the church. Eyes brimming with tears, I looked at the icons of saints that decorated the church; my gaze gravitated to a specific icon, the Mother of Jesus. *This is the Virgin Mary who sits elegantly on the left side of the iconostasis,* which, in Orthodox churches, is a screen that stands before the altar. *She is,* I thought, *so sad and beautiful, affectionately holding her Son Jesus on her breast and loving him. She is the Mother of All People, and I want her to be my mother also!* Papavasile, our loving priest, must have expressed this thought in a sermon. It was soothing, and I felt very special that I could be the Virgin Mary's son. *Everybody needs a mother who looks like Mary in the icon,* I thought.

Time and again, I came back for Sunday services, stood still in front of this icon, and prayed. I was sure she could hear my heart thudding. I often wondered if any of the churchgoers could hear it. Mary must know if my mother is dead or alive. She must know if my mother is still in America and plans to come back someday to take care of me. One Sunday, when all the people had left, I was still standing before the icon. Papavasile approached me quietly. His bearded face had a serious look, intense but not lacking fatherly love.

"I see sadness in your face," Papavasile said, obviously knowing the truth about Mother. "Our Lord's Mother is the only one who understands and comforts us. She protects the oppressed, visits the sick and those in pain, and helps the motherle—," but he didn't finish the word. "Give me your hand," he said.

I placed my hand in the priest's enormous palm. It was warm. He squeezed my hand and said, "When Jesus was dying on the cross, he looked at one of his disciples and said, 'John, this is your mother.' Then he turned to Mary and said, 'Mother, this is your son.' Do you know what Jesus meant?"

Silently, I shook my head.

Cupping his other hand over mine, Papavasile pointed to the icon. "'This is your mother.' It means that she is your mother and my mother and the mother of all humanity. It was our Lord's wish that we all have Mary as our mother. Now remember to repeat *This is my mother* each time you see her icon or when you say your prayers."

I repeated that line mentally three times before leaving the church that day. On the way out, I felt lighter. Something familiar and strangely comforting happened as I listened to my heart beating, and I made the sign of the cross over it. It was at that moment that I adopted Mother Church as a symbolic mother and sought opportunities to be a part of her, either serving as an altar boy or singing in the choir. I was fascinated by the church's melodic ritual, artistic iconography, poetic language, and chant of its priests and bishops. My life was now mapped out. *Some day, I vowed to myself, I want be a priest like Papavasile.*

Lessons I Have Learned

- A child, regardless of how young, is a person who also has feelings and a mind, although not fully developed. As painful as death or any crisis may appear to adults, the child among them must be told the truth in terms that can be understood. Even for the loss of a mother or father or significant other, the child

9

should be told. Finding out the truth at a later date causes doubt, lack of trust, and disbelief. Probably well-intentioned parents try to spare a child's feelings by lying, but as the truth surfaces, grief is accentuated by anger, and the period of unstable emotional condition is prolonged.

- Afraid of being abandoned, children repress their feelings, mistrust the adult world, and shut out their misery to avoid hurting. As a result, they act out in school and find overt or covert ways to express hostile feelings. Inwardly, they suffer. When they are not nurtured by motherly love, a false self emerges. They begin to live a pretend-life, repress feelings, comply with the expectations of their environment, and agree and accept what others offer in order to gain crumbs of love. But a life of external compliance can become one of internal defiance, resulting in chronic conflict, anxiety, fear, confusion, emptiness, and unhappiness.

- The most beautiful word on the lips of mankind is the word *mother*, and the most melodic human sound is a call from a *mother*. It is a word full of hope and love, a sweet and kind voice coming from the depths of the heart. The mother is everything—she is our consolation in sorrow, our hope in misery, and our strength in weakness. She is the source of love, mercy, sympathy, and forgiveness. When we lose our mothers, their invisible presence continues to bless and guard us constantly.

- As we try to analyze the concept of mother, it is like analyzing the existence of God. Both are mysteries and both require faith. When we think of God, we perceive him as a caring Father, Creator of all visible and invisible things, Sustainer of the Universe. We may name the attributes of God as love, compassion, energy, forgiveness, justice, and power—forces that keep the universe in motion and in harmony—making our hearts tick and keeping us alive. *What is a mother?* An instant response may be: *She is a source of love and care. She is God's right hand on earth. She is a co-creator and sustainer of a smaller universe, the family. Without her presence, there would be no life on this planet.*

- Children who lose their mother at an early age suffer perhaps the greatest loss of their lives. No one— no surrogate mother, no stepmother, or no other significant adult—can fill the abysmal gap that the absence of a mother creates. The motherless child, who might have the most loving life among well-intentioned relatives, still looks for a mother figure. On rare occasions, a resolution occurs—a mothering figure comes along and fills the gap for a while.

- In her novel *The Secret Life of Bees,* Sue Monk Kidd, through the voice of August, a loving black woman, offers a comforting thought on the concept of mother. Lily, a young girl who lost her mother early in her life, is determined to find out the truth of how her mother died. Holding Lily's hand, August says, "You have to find a mother inside yourself. We all do. Even if we already have a mother, we still have to find this part of ourselves inside. She is the power inside you, you understand? Not only the power but the love."

Additional Thoughts

From the child of five to myself is but a step. But from the newborn baby to the child of five is an appalling distance.
—Leo Tolstoy

Children's *attitudes* come to them from their need to adapt to their environment and to the diverse human condition, not merely from their need to attune themselves to the whims of the adult world.

The situation of children, because of their smallness and slow development, is an impossible one; they have to fashion their own defenses against the world in which they live, and they have to find a way of surviving in it.

2

Facing Tomorrow

Like a trapeze artist, the young person in the middle of vigorous motion must let go of his safe hold of childhood and reach out for a firm grasp of adulthood, relying on a breathless moment between the past and the future, and of those he must let go of, and those who will "receive" him.

—Erik H. Erikson

A plant, a tree, and an animal can survive in spite of harmful environmental conditions. Likewise, human beings survive in spite of hardships, difficulties, emotional deprivations, and traumas. These adversaries sculpt character, shape personalities, and sharpen survival skills.

In the middle of September 1932, I found myself at school in a class of first graders. I was seated at a desk next to George Tsakiris, a chubby boy with blond hair and blue eyes. The teacher, a plump woman of about thirty, smelled of perfume and always held in her right hand a thin stick from an olive tree. Eulalia was a strict teacher who never left unpunished the slightest mischief in class. The second week of school, she demonstrated her disciplinary skill when she observed Tsakiris munching fried potato peels while she was reading us a story. Eulalia whacked each hand six times with her stick, leaving red welts on Tsakiris' oily palms. My poor friend bit his lips in defiant silence. That scene transmitted fear to all of us and stayed with us for as long as we were around her; it also enabled me to obey her every command, so terrified was I of being a target of her wrath.

That winter was cold and damp. Tsakiris and I entertained ourselves by making paper boats and letting them sail down little rivulets. My shoes were always wet, and perhaps for this reason I often caught a cold. Toasty under the covers, I awaited Katerina's homemade medicine. This was one of the few times I was aware that she paid attention to me. It was a new experience to feel cared for. I felt awkward, for I sensed I was in the way, although she was benevolently compassionate toward me when I had a cold. But her eyes conveyed the message: *No more staying home and being sick. I want you out of bed and in school.*

The following year we had a different teacher; she was a tall brunette with wavy hair and thick eyebrows over her dark eyes. Theodora (meaning "God's gift") had renounced married life and dedicated herself to teaching God's children. Each day she started her class with a prayer. As well as being a general classroom teacher, she also taught drama. She loved her students and was particularly patient with those who had learning disabilities. I was sure she loved me. *If I were older, I would marry her,* I thought. In class I was attentive to her every word, and I felt strong ties to her growing in me. I was beside myself with joy when the following year she assigned me the major role in a school play. Then I fell incurably in love with her and kept having dreams in which she and I were the same age and were friends.

The play was based on a historic event that took place in 1821 when, after four hundred years, the Greek nation was liberated from the yoke of the Ottoman Turks. The plot described how the Turks captured a Greek hero, Athanasios Diakos, and subjected him to horrible tortures. They tried to force him to deny his faith in Christ and to worship Allah. Athanasios refused to accept the Muhammadan religion. As a result the Turks burned him alive, slowly, on a skewer.

I played the part of Athanasios, and Theodora coached me. I felt like the luckiest guy in her class. Within the four weeks of intense rehearsals, I internalized the martyr's agonizing death. I could feel his pain. Suffering appealed to me. At home, I was diligent in rehearsing my lines, and as I looked in the mirror, I no longer saw myself, for looking back at me was the mighty warrior Athanasios Diakos.

14

After the performance, as the audience applauded, Theodora hugged me and kissed my forehead. She grabbed my hand and lifted it high as though I were an Olympic champion. I must have done justice to the play, for the audience gave me a standing ovation. On that memorable day, I grew five inches taller, and I was the most important person in the world.

Until I reached my teen years, I held a special admiration in my heart for Athanasios' courage. He was my hero, and I believed that some day I would go down in history as he had. Under all circumstances, I would defend my faith, even if I had to suffer a martyr's death. I apparently gained vicarious satisfaction through playing the part of a victim of hate, injustice, and cruel torture.

My desire to become a hero led me, for a while, to erroneous beliefs: that I must renounce the fact I was a teenager with fantasies of grandiosity and power; that no longer could I fear death and humiliation; that I must be willing to go through trials and, if necessary, give up my life for others. Fortunately, the simple wisdom of my friend Tsakiris brought me back to sanity. He said, "We can admire heroes and be strong, but we don't need to become heroes in order to be men." Years later, I came to realize that mythical heroes, war heroes, sports heroes, and superstars are meant to inspire us to find the potential within our own soul. They waken something inside us, something of our own, making us aware of a special strength that our Creator gives to every human being. If we choose certain heroes to be our very own role models, their voices can encourage and inspire us to see in our character the good aspects that we admire in them.

Meanwhile, as the culture of the island seeped into my psyche, I turned my attention to my own affairs. I could not take the whole world in one bite, as a giant could, but I could gnaw small manageable pieces as a beaver does. I used all kinds of techniques known as "character defenses." Among my peers, my being motherless had faded from their vocabulary, and they called me the *Americanaki,* "the little American," a title that I cherished for many years. I learned not to expose myself—feelings and thoughts and sometimes actions—not to stand out lest I lose even one friend. I wanted everybody to love me.

15

Deep down, I wanted a special girl to love me, and out of seven good-looking girls in my class, I chose Eleni because she was the prettiest. I don't think she knew my feelings. I wanted her for myself, and I did not want any of the other boys getting too friendly with her. I thought of her often, and periodically I would secretly slip a loving note into her school bag, hoping she would read it.

Unfortunately, on Easter Sunday of that year, her father died and Eleni went into mourning. She wore black and seldom smiled. I attended her father's funeral and offered my condolences. Her tearful eyes looked at me with pain. She probably missed the presence of her father, like I missed my mother. I discussed the matter with my friend Tsakiris and with no one else, for I was afraid of being teased.

I had to plunge ahead compulsively to conform with the ways of the world with grim equanimity. School and play with my friends kept me out of the house. Summers were sweet but short; winters were long and gloomy. At home, with my siblings asleep, dinners were quiet, and I did not say much or eat much. Katerina would break the silence to talk about her children, and my father would respond in a laconic manner: "Great...Nice....Really?... That's very funny....I had a hard day today and I need to rest." Then he would withdraw to the couch and read the newspaper. As for me, I repressed any feelings I had. I did not think it mattered to them what I thought or felt. However, what I did outside the house mattered to them. Their concern was about maintaining the family's good name, its good reputation.

My parents' bedroom was adjacent to mine, and at night I could hear Katerina and my father whispering about me. "He's a troubled child," my stepmother would say. "I don't know how to deal with him anymore." She did not reveal how she dealt with me in my father's absence, using a stick on my back and threatening me: "If you tell your father, I will kill you."

Time and again, I saw her killing stray cats that happened to cross our yard. I believed she was capable of killing me, too, and I kept my mouth sealed. I tried to make my presence unobtrusive, but it was hard for her to cope with me in addition to her own demanding children. Angry and frustrated, she directed her pent-up emotions toward me. In her eyes I was worthless. Nothing that I did pleased her. I often considered running away.

After school hours, Tsakiris and I climbed a little mountain in the outskirts of Moria where the breeze was soothing and the fields were arrayed in colorful flowers. On the way back home, we made a ball out of rags and kicked it around, pretending we were soccer stars. When Tsakiris was not around, I roamed alone by the river and climbed a steep hill to watch the sunset. The sun slipped behind the distant mountaintops as I gazed in ecstasy. Listening to the mystical whispering of the trees and the monotonous lapping of the river, I discovered the peace and tranquility of nature. The movements of the clouds created images that brought a shiver to my spine. As the sky darkened, the chirping of the birds soothed my loneliness. Before darkness fell, I hurried home to prepare for the evening ritual of "parental presence."

Sometimes after dinner, my father would hum a little tune, and humming would change into a word or two, but he never finished even a part of a song. He would recline in his favorite chair, and with a silent nod, he would signal that it was time for bed. His order had to be obeyed.

Although most of the parents of the area forbade their children to go swimming unsupervised, many of the kids paid little heed and spent most of the summer splashing about. The sea was two kilometers away from the village. One day, Tsakiris and I decided to join some other friends. When I returned home, Katerina took a look at my face and touched it with her index finger. Salty! When she realized where I had been, her face turned red with increasing hostility and aggression. "I know where you've been, you prodigal son." She picked up her stick from behind the door and hit me across the shoulders, barking that I was too frail and too young to go swimming and that I was a disobedient, rebellious child. "If you get sick again, I'll let you rot in bed."

It was bewildering to me to observe how grown-ups punished and rewarded; sometimes they employed the direct use of authority, and sometimes they used subtle and devious methods. A child's right to express his own identity and grow as a unique person was stifled by loud, demanding expressions, by sweet manipulating words, or by corporal punishment. Katerina chose

17

a stick to discipline me, a common form of punishment used by teachers in those days. They called it the "holy stick that came from paradise." The sight of the stick terrified me. But more painful than any physical pain was Katerina's determination to restrain and deny me the freedom to be a growing boy.

Frightened by her anger at my swimming in the sea, even Kiki and Jimmy cried, begging her to stop. Her reaction was to become more angry. "Shut up," she shouted at them and continued hitting me until I was sprawled on the ground. Unable to escape, my blood rose to my head and my temples throbbed. Slowly, I stood up and swung a fierce blow at her chest. Shocked at my rage, holding her breast with both hands, she cursed the day she had accepted me into her life. But she pulled back and never touched me again.

My father finally showed up and, of course, took Katerina's side. He told me that I was responsible for Mamma's anger, that I was stubborn, and that I did not do what I was told. He elaborated, saying that Mamma loved me and I should obey her words. If I did whatever she told me to do and respected her, there would not be any problem. Further, I had no business going swimming; I was still too young, and she had the right to punish me. Should I dare to touch Mamma again, then I would find out from him what real punishment was.

This tragic episode brought about my final separation from Katerina. Lacking significant emotional and personal involvement with her, I at last broke away from her dominance. She in turn shut the door of her heart in my face. She withdrew her love in such a rigid way that I felt she would never love me again. In later years, even in my adult life, I wondered, *How did I end up with so many negative feelings about myself? At what point did things go haywire?*

It was evident that Katerina would never understand me or realize how frightened I was when she was angry with me. I wanted to be a boy like other boys; I wanted to be more manly, but her concern about me prevented me from growing up. When she disapproved, I felt like a naughty little boy. My fear was that Mamma would take my manhood away. Yet what if she stopped loving me?

Today, as a therapist, I smile compassionately when I see strong and successful men become frightened children in the face of a woman's anger. "Hell has no fury like a woman who is even slightly disgruntled." We start life as helpless, fragile infants, dependent on our mother's willingness to hold us and care for us even though we are selfish creatures. We demand her unconditional love, and we fear she may abandon us and leave us to die. When we become adults, we realize that we are not worthy of all the care and emotional investment that we have received from our mothers. The fear of many men is that either their girlfriend or wife may discover that they are not the omnipotent heroes they pretend to be. The fear compounds with the neurotic thought: *What if my woman leaves me for a better man? It could happen.*

At times, when I saw mothers caring for their children or playing with them, my heartbeat increased. The grief over my mother's death, which I had repressed by becoming involved in activities, would then resurge in its pure essence: *Mommy, why did you have to die? Now I have nobody to love me.* Even today I still wonder what happens to children who lose a parent, especially their mother. Perhaps an even more difficult question is, can anything ever fill the gap left by this loss?

The animal whose mother dies continues with life placidly and grows among other animals of its kind, oblivious of the loss. The knowledge of death is self-reflective and conceptual, and animals are spared such ponderings. They live, and they disappear with the same thoughtlessness; a few minutes of fear, a few seconds of anguish, and it is over.

In the village, the gruesome sight of animals being killed—chickens, goats, lambs, rabbits—was normal. Death for animals meant food for humans—a strange power of the living. I never thought my father would kill a pet rabbit for our Sunday dinner; yet he did, and the whole family enjoyed that tasty meal. I learned to ignore the reality of slaughtering innocent animals so that humans can have food, and tried not to think about it.

On my birthday, Tsakiris gave me a slingshot. The first time I used it, I shot a swallow. I saw the little bird slowly expiring, and I began to cry. *It was a terrible crime. I had no reason to kill an innocent creature. Would God ever forgive me?* Guilt began to carve a sensitive area in my inner self. Its effect served to remind me to have respect for life.

19

Springtime arrived, making life in the village more enjoyable. During Lent, the church was the center of activity for the whole community, and Holy Week was a time for young and old to relive the last days of the life of Christ. The most dramatic hour occurred the night before Good Friday; lights were turned off and the church was enveloped in total darkness. A procession of lit tapers and burning incense took place, and the priest, carrying a crucifix, chanted in a grieving voice: "Today, hangs on a tree, the One who suspended the earth amid the waters." The choir members, including Tsakiris and myself, sang mournful melodies, and waves of people fell upon their knees, wailing. The grieving crowd turned St. Basil's Church into the city of Jerusalem at the time of Christ's crucifixion.

Upon seeing Christ on the cross, I could not restrain my tears. To me, it was not an image of a human body fastened to plywood. It was the real body of Christ nailed to the cross; it was the Son of God, whose pain I felt in my own body. My involvement in his passion elicited pity in me. I feared a similar fate might befall me. But the priest explained that it was the violations and sins of the people that brought about the crucifixion. Christ's suffering on the cross paid the price for our sins.

Hearing about the true meaning of the passion and knowing that we would soon celebrate Easter, Christ's resurrection, my sadness turned to joy. I was restored by this vicarious brush with destruction and death and then with the resurrection and new life. I did not die. Feeling forgiven and alive, I was no longer afraid of death. Now I could face tomorrow and the many tomorrows afterward with hope and courage. I could celebrate this newness of life with faith, with joyful anticipation, and with confidence.

Lessons I Have learned

- Growing children need constant attention. When another child enters the family, the older children, who formerly were the center of attention, feel neglected. Sibling rivalry causes insecurity and jealousy. When children interpret the change in the composition of the family as a lessening of parental love for them, they seek love from other sources. Parents are not perfect, and their imperfections influence the lives of their children.

- Children who are not allowed to express their feelings—either because of the many *don'ts* and *shouldn'ts* of the adult world around them or because of their fear of being punished and rejected—eventually display physical or emotional symptoms. Some of them are constantly sick and have to visit the doctor frequently. Others display neurotic behavior, obsessions, addictions, even violence.

- In school, children discover they are not the center of attention. They have to learn and play with a large and diverse group of human beings. A teacher's positive or negative approach to children's abilities reinforces already-existing attitudes that children inherit from their parents or parental figures.

- Peer relationships are significant for growing children. In their interactions with their peers, children learn to test the ideas and values given them by their parents, and sometimes the results are less than desirable. If children do not receive sufficient attention and love at home, they allow themselves to be swayed and led by friends in ways that can be harmful.

- In mimesis, or mimicry, a child can internalize both the good and bad habits, attitudes, and behaviors of someone else—such as a parent or significant other, a hero or a villain. Thus they may negate their own true personality. Mimicking is part of human growth; gradually children reshape, refine, and adapt their mimicking to meet their own needs.

- Children who at an early age lose their mother or father either by death or divorce suffer an emotional trauma which effects are carried into their adult life. Anger, emptiness, insecurity, lack of trust, and other

negative symptoms become part of their life and stifle their growth and maturity. Subconsciously, they
are always in search of an idealized loving mother. A
ray of hope diffuses the loss when the motherless
adult finds a loving mate, an affectionate spouse, or
a caring friend.

Additional Thoughts

Biological parents, single parents, adoptive parents, close relatives, and guardians are human, not perfect. As their children
develop, parents make changes in their own lives, some complex
and others simple. Some of these transitions result in joyful feelings; others cause sadness that influences the children's lives.

Meanwhile, children continue to grow and experience their
own transitions. They make choices that may not necessarily follow parental advice or directives, yet it is important to recognize
that the children themselves own their choices. Their experiences
are greatly influenced by education, ethnicity, and culture—as
may be manifested in their actions, dress, behavior, and the way
they think and feel. Eventually, children become adults, and
each one designs and starts a unique journey, guided mainly by
the inner self.

3

Freedom

The survival within us is unfathomable. The potential for healing damaged emotions is great if we do not hinder it with negative thoughts and destructive behavior.
—Harriet Stratstein, PhD

While growing up among the gigantic olive trees that bordered the little town of Moria, I did not remain idle. Reaching through the branches for the olives made my arms grow longer, and sorting the harvest by hand made my fingernails firm. I became an expert at stretching my limbs and sorting olives. My father, the proud olive-grove owner, watched the freshly pressed oil being stored in steel barrels. Smiling, he would say to me, "Someday this oil will pay for your education." Even in my early years, he had plans for me. As an American, he could not tolerate the idea of his son making a career of olive picking. He wanted me to become a doctor, a wish that haunted me each time a thorn got under my nail as I sorted the olives spread out over the arid ground. Obviously he had regrets that he had taken me to Greece; and to add to his disappointment, Katerina did not want to go to America. So my exile in Greece continued.

Hardly a day passed that my father did not tell me how much he missed America, his secret love.

"Every morning, the moment I wake up, I see the American flag in front of my eyes, waving, caressing my face, and I visualize the big buildings, broad streets, and busy people rushing to work."

Eventually he persuaded Katerina that it would be of financial benefit to the family if he returned to America for a couple years, worked hard, and sent money to her to support the family. "That's where the money is, and that's where I want to be." He called the United States the *promised land.*

In September 1937, before the harvesting of the olives, my father bade us farewell and returned to the country of his dreams. The absent-father syndrome added to my loneliness. I was sad, for I missed having him around. I accepted the fact that I had no real mother; now I felt that life had also cheated me out of a father. Other kids of my age had parents who cared about them. Katerina, to serve her own needs, tried to make me feel important; she called me "the man of the house." I liked the title, but her increasing expectations made me spend less time at home and more time at the marketplace observing the adult population. Of course I craved to be important and to feel admired. I had a need to excel and be accepted by my peers.

Being at liberty to entertain myself, I got into the habit of spending time in Alexis' tavern where, unknown to Katerina, I learned to drink ouzo and eat octopus with some of my peers, mainly George Tsakiris. Even now, I can visualize Alexis—a short, jovial man, the personification of mischief—carrying a sizzling octopus on a ceramic platter and pouring out glasses of ouzo. With my mouth drooling in expectation, I would cut a tender tentacle, savor it slowly, and wash it down with ouzo. Peak moments like that were times when I wished Eleni could see me. I could drink ouzo and even dance like an adult. That's the taste of my teen years. Even now, I can close my eyes, breathe deeply, and recall the smell, the bold, fecund aroma of the Aegean Sea, exquisite and sensual, the fragrance of Greece, old and new, in a lasting orgasm of springtime. Enjoying the openness of traditional Greek character, the zest for life evident in social affairs and parties, I felt alive. The parties were always flavored with humor, laughter, serious conversations, satire, singing, and dancing.

Observing older people, specifically men, I was fascinated by their style and character. Along with their ouzo and wine, they devoured fragrant hors d'oeuvres, and they danced, sang, and laughed loudly. Carefree, they satisfied themselves with everyday pleasures. Their spirit stemmed from their ancestors' philosophy: "Eat, drink, and be merry, for tomorrow we die." But tomorrow was never an issue. In the men's noble simplicity, I sensed a silent greatness. My deep yearning was to be one of them someday, and I thought, *Why does adulthood take such a long time in coming?*

Watching and listening to adults in their mid-twenties and early thirties and realizing they still had no direction in their lives, I wondered what was to become of me when *I* grew up. I felt inferior. My school demanded that I had to be good, virtuous, and wise. Fragments of Papavasile's sermons slowly penetrated my teen mind:

"Do not waste precious time. Avoid idle talk...Show respect for your elders...Be grateful for what you have and don't whine about what you don't have...Be openhearted, loving, patient, and generous...Be aware of your thoughts. If you want to be without emotional pain, fill your heart with painless thoughts...If you want to be happy, learn to smile...Walk with straight shoulders, and look life fearlessly in the face. Do not surrender to waves of random worries...Keep Christ in your heart and cherish his loving presence in your life."

Like a mosaic, my life was gradually taking form, a mixture of Alexis, the free-spirited man, and Papavasile, the spiritual giant: a vital challenge between reality and idealism.

Now, as I look back with an adult mind, I find increasing appreciation for my years spent in Greece. It was a segment of my history that taught me many valuable lessons and put my life in perspective. Any country, any culture, provides an environment that shapes the human character. Life in Greece was not terrific, but it was not terrible because it provided a synthesis of spirit and intelligence.

Growing up with a stepmother and feeling unloved was not an ideal mother-son relationship. Gradually, however, I came to realize my stepmother was a woman who did care; otherwise I would have died in early childhood. She did not have to love me, but she chose to show me reasonable care. My part was to live by her rules. All humans have to learn to live by rules to survive, and if I wanted to be loved by her, I had to be lovable.

Between placating Katerina and leveling her power, I chose to cooperate with her wishes, a discipline that made me feel stronger. I learned to play with Kiki and Jimmy, and being older, I became their keeper. I began to see them not as stepbrother and stepsister but as my own sister and brother, and I loved them dearly. As I involved myself with them, I no longer resented their presence, and seeing us happy together, my stepmother became more loving to me and treated me as a son of her own flesh and blood.

It took me a long time to realize that she was basically a good, loving, and moral person. From her, I learned some of my ethical principles: Be kind to other people. Be concerned about the misfortune of others—the poor, the disabled, the elderly. Be honest. Be truthful. Be generous to the less fortunate. When you are kind to others, you receive kindness back. These traits were instilled in me during my growing years, and all of my adult life I have tried to be mindful of the needs of others.

What was of special significance to me was the gradual realization of the good deeds Katerina did and how she did them. She never made a display and never let her good deeds be known. For example, at one end of our village, a poverty-stricken, elderly widow, Amalia, lived alone in an old hut. Just before our family dinnertime, Katerina, with a tender smile, would say to me: "Take this dish of food to Amalia while it's still warm. There's no need to tell anybody where you're going. This is our secret." There was something magical in her voice that gave me a feeling of joy as I followed her instructions. Her daily act of kindness was reaching out to help the poor without expecting anything in return. She had no need of praise, nor did she boast of her good works. Her reward came from the knowledge that a hungry woman ate the food she had prepared. The joy she gave to Amalia became her own great joy. Katerina's frequent and surreptitious generosity left a lifelong mark on me.

Saturdays were appropriated for charity. Katerina's home was a little center for the hungry and homeless. Any poor person who knocked at her door was given a thick slice of homemade bread, a handful of olives, a piece of cheese, or a little bottle of virgin olive oil. No one left Katerina's presence empty-handed.

Her generosity came from a special place, from a compassionate heart where her soul lived.

Generosity and kindness were aspects of her spirit, and they were carried out without any thought of compensation. It was a quality of her soul that expressed kindness, beneficence, and sacrificial giving. Even if there was only one loaf of bread in our house, not enough for our family of five, part of it would go to the hungry. At times, there was hardly enough money to cover our expenses, and yet, when someone asked for help, Katerina would give from her small jar of savings. She said,

"The giving of money is not enough. Many people who give willingly do not give because they have wealth to give. They give because they obey their heart's voice. We all have something to give; it may not be a grand gift, but no matter how small, what we share suffices when it comes from our heart."

I am fortunate that my wife, Pat, possesses loving principles similar to those of Katerina. Throughout our married life, Pat has always bestowed many kindnesses upon individuals and families. She willingly gives of her time to those needing comfort and does favors for those who find themselves in a bind. Every week, Pat sets aside a tasty meal for a hungry soul. Over the years, every other Tuesday she makes a special dish for a group of twelve poor people who have fallen on hard times. She cherishes the effort and smiles when she engages me to deliver the "goodies."

Lessons I Have Learned

- Misfortunes are our common lot. The loss of a parent, a child, or other loved one causes lasting pain. The grieving person needs both patience and time for healing to take place, and then more patience and time to determine a new direction to take. An emotionally deprived person may need additional support from a compassionate adult.

- Parents, culture, education, and peer associations not only influence human development but also "program" it. Daily, growing children absorb or imitate experiences from their immediate environment. Most parents are aware that, directly or indirectly, they program their children to follow their example and let them know they are expected to excel in life. School, peer pressure, societal expectations, and mass media forge or stifle already-existing patterns.

- In every human being there are positive and negative characteristics. Socrates once said, "No person is knowingly bad." If we believe that good and evil walk parallel to each other and that anyone can be good or bad, then we have choices. We can choose the better part of ourselves, try to perform good actions, and avoid evil.

- Even the most evil person, beyond any doubt, has dormant good qualities. If we stop judging what appears to be evil and look deeper, we may discover another side of that person. This other side would be worth considering if our attitude toward that person were positive. There is no evil without its equivalent good.

- Generosity and kindness are activities of our soul. If we act in a kind and generous manner because we have ulterior motives if we feel obligated or we wish to be recognized, we really have no feelings of compassion and love; therefore, our generosity and kindness are of little substantial value. Generosity and kindness are ramifications of love that give of themselves without any expectation of material reward. This is a giving that grants true freedom.

- Acts of kindness and generosity need to be done with sensitivity and within the boundaries of reality. Excessive and unexamined kindness and generosity may make the recipient irresponsible and dependent. Healthy efforts of reaching out require discretion and wise direction. One of the objectives of philanthropic efforts should focus on the idea of helping others to help themselves.

Additional Thoughts

How are we formed and transformed? Most of our behaviors are built into us from external sources, often from interaction with others who deal only with our physical presence. These sources and interactions are what give us a "self" and a superego. Our whole world of right and wrong, good and bad, our identity, precisely who we are—all these are grafted onto us by others— parents, teachers, peers—and thus the truly authentic part of most human beings is stifled.

If we feel insecure in some areas and see others as being superior or having control over our lives, or if we worry about being criticized, we need to consider that these individuals have insecurities of their own and may be projecting them onto us. With the exception of God, no one really knows anything about our inner self, our spiritual dimension, the divine part of us. Even we know ourselves only partially.

We should not compare ourselves with others or live anyone else's life. As we mature, we discover who we really are, we accept the truth about ourselves, and we make responsible decisions. A well-lived, balanced life that avoids excesses can be a happier and healthier life.

4

Independence

A man learns masculinity primarily from his father. But generations of boys who grow up without caring fathers or male mentors to emulate are left to guess what "men" are really like. They rely on cultural icons—larger-than-life images—as models of masculinity. —Frank Pittman, MD

On the brink of World War II, in September 1939, my father returned to Lesvos. He had been gone two years. He was proud he had crossed the Atlantic on a ship flying the American flag. Soon after his return, he tried to exercise his authority over me. He was constantly on my back with endless questions: "Where were you? When was the last time you took a bath? How are you doing in school? I haven't seen you at your books lately. You stay out until all hours of the night. I'd like to know who you're hanging around with." I detested his questions and answered them vaguely.

When my father was at home, he did not impress me as a model of masculinity that I could draw upon. He was the patriarch, sitting in his special chair, criticizing and pontificating. He was a source of irritation to me, and I perceived him as weak. When he lost control of himself over my behavior, his rage knew no bounds; his face would turn fiery red, and he would strike me with his belt. Such scenes remained with me many years after my emancipation from parental ties.

Fearing that his anger might cause him to drop dead of a coronary, Katerina took his side and tried to pacify him. She turned against me. When she was alone with him at dinner or in the bedroom, she admitted her inability to deal with her own growing children, as well as with me. In spite of her attitude, I viewed my relationship with her as supportive and nonthreatening. My father was like a fourth child. Katerina babied him and called him "my lord." If I failed in anything, she would say, "Wait until *the lord* comes home," implying punishment. I hated to hear it.

Troublesome as life was with my stepmother, it was preferable to the third degree my father put me through. At this point, my relationship with Katerina was more favorable than that with my father, so the situation made it easier for me to display hostility and anger toward him. I wonder if he sensed he was being displaced if he felt jealous because of the affection I was giving to his wife. Or maybe he realized I was growing up and becoming independent.

Besides antagonizing him and then feeling manly, I also felt terror when he got angry. By staying out late and disobeying his orders, I drove him to behave like a lunatic. I thought he would kill me. He threatened to sell the bike I had bought with money he had sent me from America. I tested my limits with Katerina. I could push her too far and get my own way, but I was not able to get the better of my father. He expected me to behave as an adult. When I failed to meet his expectations, he called me "incapable and worthless," an image that took me years to erase. Perhaps he was struggling with his own past life that could have blocked his understanding of a teenager. I was not his "dream" son. Gradually he withdrew his love for me. He cared only for Jimmy and Kiki and his wife, Katerina, I thought. Obviously through these turbulent teen years, I could not see him as a benevolent father who would unconditionally accept or even condone my defiant behavior.

Later in my life, after years of training in psychology, I came to realize that the father-son relationship is by definition a sensitive one. My father's angry outbursts were not necessarily a reaction to my teen behavior. It was evident, by the way he talked to me, that I was a challenge to his parental authority. It was also a hidden dance for my mother's attention, the unconscious attempts to gain her favor and be her hero. Does any human being of any age ever transcend the desire to be mothered and genuinely loved?

The seeming impossibility of resolving the broken link with him promoted my friendship with Alexis, who became my mentor. My father tried to stop me from going to Alexis' tavern. "It's bad for the reputation of our family," he said. "You are too young to be frequenting taverns. You are wasting your time there." Home became an arena where issues could not be worked out. When the school day ended, we spent the afternoon playing soccer, and then my friends and I proceeded to Alexis' tavern. Alexis offered something vital: the picture of competent masculinity. There was nothing he could not do. Besides telling us heroic stories of his younger years and giving us a drink of ouzo, he was a father and mentor to me and my friends. He was the image of an older man, a mentor and father: overly driven and experienced, smart and accomplished, successful and sensitive, qualities that I secretly admired.

I really wished to act bravely and to courageously attempt to bring about peace in the family. I did not want to be thought of as the black sheep. Tension and outbursts of anger stifled my vitality. Noticing my periodic nervousness, Alexis said, "You told me how angry you are at your father and how strict he is with you. You are a fine young man, but you need to reconcile with your father, so these outbursts at home can stop." Alexis was right. I needed my father's love and support. Besides, who else could possibly provide passage for me to America, the promised land!?

If I were to reconcile with my father and earn his love, I had to do my part, yet I was not sure what to do. I started paying him silent homage. Although I had no desire to be like him, outside home I followed his ethic of hard work. I spent long hours in our olive groves and, like an adult, learned how to harvest the ripe olives, to prune trees, and to chop wood for our fireplace. Eventually I took care of our animals: a donkey, three goats, and a dog. Noticing my involvement, Dad nodded favorably to Katerina. *He's growing up, finally.*

My father and I never had a real relationship. We never had the friendship I longed for. He was not a bad man, but he did not know how to show his emotions. Perhaps *his* father had not been available to him. One cold day I came home carrying a heavy load of firewood on my shoulders and perspiring profusely. It was the first time I ever saw my father smile with approval at something I'd done. He actually turned around and said, "That's pretty heavy! How did you manage to carry all this? Let me help you unload." I was fourteen years old.

My yearning to reconcile with my father never became reality. I had great support from Papavasile, our priest, and I had a close relationship with Alexis, a relationship that my father probably envied. A combination of these two men fulfilled my wish for an idealized father. The priest's influence was subtle yet strong. His church rituals were recreation for me. He taught me how to chant, which made me feel important, and the church became the center of my soul. Also, it was the only place where Eleni, my first love, could see me and hear me chanting.

One Sunday when Papavasile told the story of the prodigal son, how father and son embraced and reconciled, I saw tears in his eyes. He smiled and said, "The angels in heaven rejoice when reconciliation takes place and love prevails between father and son." Did Papavasile aim his sermon as a subtle lesson for me? *Like the prodigal son, return to your father and rediscover his love for you.*

I always called Papavasile *Father.* Because he loved what he believed, I enjoyed listening to him. He was a good storyteller, making even old stories come to life. On one occasion when he asked me to read to the congregation the First Epistle of Paul to the Corinthians, chapter 13, he took me aside after the service and spoke to me about the power of love: "Love believes, hopes, endures everything. Love never fails." It was a brief and stimulating explanation. Was this the kind of love a man should have for a woman? Papavasile had probably suspected that I had feelings for Eleni. He paused, looked into my eyes, and gave me a strong man's hug. A pillar of faith, this priest spoke his mind bravely. Although he did not impose his wisdom on others, he appreciated a receptive audience.

It became evident to me that the priest, whom I loved and respected, wanted me to regain my father's love. I knew Papavasile had a strong relationship with his son, Christos. (Orthodox married men are allowed to be ordained if they are already married.) I saw Papavasile playing soccer with him. He knew I needed friendship with my father as well. But then life took a radical turn.

On May 4, 1941, I was riding my bike to school, a six-kilometer stretch of road from Moria to the capital city of Lesvos, Mytilene. When the old castle of the capital came into view, I saw a strange sight. The sky-blue flag that had waved over the castle every day was gone and was replaced by a swastika. A *swastika!* In shock, I skidded to a halt. *Oh, my God, what my father and the people of Moria feared has happened. The Nazis have invaded our island!*

At school that day, our teacher Mr. Lainos spoke to us, his voice full of sadness:

"Our island succumbed to the enemy last night. Like the rest of Europe, Greece is under Hitler's yoke. But remember, the Nazis may conquer our land, but they can never conquer our spirit."

It is hard to describe the havoc that occurred three days later. Nazi soldiers harassed the innocent population. They entered houses and gathered up precious artifacts, beds and blankets, plates and silverware, tables and chairs, and piled them into their jeeps. The villagers panicked.

I returned from school to find my dad cowering in a corner of our kitchen. Beside him sat my stepmother in tears. Two Nazis were ransacking our house. One of them reached for my bike. "Leave my bike alone, you lizard-faced monster," I mumbled, scared. Indifferent to my anxiety, the soldier rode away on my bike, an arrogant look on his face.

The invaders posted yellow signs in large German script, indicating directions and names of the streets. Angry and heart-broken, one night I defied the curfew and crept through the village destroying the signs. I brought a large one home. My father's face froze with fear.

"Are you crazy? The Nazis will burn us alive if they find out you insulted them like that."

"I don't care," I said. "They took my bike away. Should I keep silent and sit on my hands?"

"You committed sabotage. Do you know what that means?"

"I hate the Nazis," I said. "I want to see them dead. My friends and I have made plans. We're going to fight them."

"I know how you feel," my father said. Then he took me into the living room and said, "I went back to America to improve the financial situation for our family. When I had saved enough money, I returned to Lesvos. Sometimes fathers have to go away to earn a living. But they never stop loving their children. Now I am here to be with you. Our times are critical, and you are a growing young man. The occupying forces do not play games. They could send you to Germany to work in their factories manufacturing weapons or to work in a concentration camp. So we have to be very careful. I ask you not to do anything so foolish again." He put his arm around my shoulders and said, "Now help me do away with this sign." He cut it into small pieces, and I put them one by one into our fireplace, watching the flames with relief. In my heart I knew he loved me.

When I became an adult and later a father, I thought of my father not as someone who was distant or who had deprived me of his approval or companionship or love. I saw him as a person who himself had been deprived of parental support. Because of poverty, he had left Greece in his early twenties and sought to make a better life in America. Although it seemed he did not behave like a father to me, at least I was grateful for his decision to settle in the New World, for I was born an American citizen. In my maturing years, I became forever grateful for his insight to make America our homeland, and I eventually returned there.

Choosing the ministry as my career, I needed to cultivate the admonitions, teachings, and virtues of Christ. If I were to teach others how to live a Christian life, a life of compassion, care, forgiveness, and love, it was important to practice what I preached. The story of the prodigal son served as a metaphor. *There is abundant love in a father's heart that sometimes-arrogant youth cannot perceive.*

Even when I returned to America, I had the urge to reconcile with my father and have a mature relationship with him. He had chosen to spend his retirement in his homeland. Reconciliation from a distance could not be done adequately by speaking over the telephone or by sending contrite letters. It had to be shown in action. So, several times during his retirement years, I visited the Greek island where he lived. Each time, our souls connected, and I felt very happy. God granted me another blessing: to see my father as a friend. On one occasion, he asked me to chant his favorite church hymn, "Holy God, Holy and Mighty, Holy and Immortal, have mercy on us," which I did, and he accompanied me in a gentle voice. The following Sunday, he came to see me at St. Basil's Church, where I used to sing in the choir. By then I was a priest and had been invited to celebrate the Liturgy there.

It was a most moving moment when I saw my father approaching the altar to receive communion. My hands began to tremble as I brought the chalice close to him, and I whispered, "The servant of God is receiving the precious Body and Blood of Christ for the remission of sins and life everlasting." There was a glowing smile on his face, and a tear rolled down his cheek. I wondered how he was feeling. Perhaps he was thinking, *Is this really my son?* After the service, he proudly introduced me to his friends: "This is Father Peter; he is my son." My father, who called *me* Father, had become my spiritual son! How was I to understand this? This was my father who loved me according to his ability to love. At last, my love for him had matured. "Dad, I love you," I said, looking into his aging eyes. "Please call me by my first name. I'm your son."

At the Greek airport the day of my return to the United States, I was deeply moved by my father's behavior. Relatives and old friends came to say goodbye. My father, with a shadow of sadness in his eyes, stood speechless next to my stepmother. I knew she loved him and would take care of him. She looked at him, and I heard her saying: "Time of separation is approaching, and our hearts are whimpering because we shall be apart again." As I kept shaking hands saying, *"Kali antamosi"* (meaning "until we meet again"), I rehearsed in my mind how I would say goodbye to my father. Finally, hugging him and kissing him on both cheeks, I whispered, "Dad, stay well. I'll be back again next summer."

One of my most beautiful memories is his affectionate response: "My son, this is the last goodbye kiss," he said, holding back his tears. "I won't be here next time. Don't worry about my absence." He smiled. "My life is complete now. Continue your life in America, the country of your birth. Be the best that you can. Promise me that you will come back again. This is where a part of your younger years started. This is where you learned the first lessons of life. This could be another source of strength for you."

"Dad, you will be here, and we'll celebrate," I said, feeling uneasy, knowing that his smile served to disguise his emotions. I wanted to hold on to him with all the power and tenderness of the boy I had been when I first left the island, but I remained silent, holding his hand. The eloquent preacher of the Gospel could not find the few comforting words that my heart yearned to say. His premonition, *I won't be here next time,* was hard to accept.

As the plane moved down the runway, I could barely see faces and hands waving farewell. My father's silhouette faded fast, but his image was sharp in my heart. Soaring high over the Aegean Sea, I made an effort to glean some fragments of wisdom from my experiences over the few decades since my original departure from the island. But life is a deep mystery and it takes more than logic to understand it. Life is always presenting us with new challenges and mysteries that we cannot comprehend.

On my way back to the United States, memories, like a long string of worry beads, went through my head. It was time to face reality. I knew I would be with my own family the following day, and there was the possibility I would be a better father than my own. I also had to continue my responsibilities as the spiritual father to my congregation. The ministry is always a mystery. It is only with faith and trust in a loving God that we discover his plan for us, and what needs to be done. Our faith in him enables us to pursue his plan in the best way humanly possible.

Today, as I think of my father, I am at peace with his presence in my life. I wonder how much of my deprivation was caused willfully by him, and how much was not of his will. To what degree was he aware or unaware of his contact with me and his influence on me? I began to see him as a human being, an imperfect father—like other imperfect fathers, including myself—who, under the circumstances, tried to do the best he could.

Amazingly, his premonition *I won't be here next time* proved to be accurate. In my next visit to the island, he was no longer there. During the winter of that same year, because of a severe attack of pneumonia, he died. It is God's design of the human body to die. But in reality, as we depart from this life, we continue to live in the presence of God and in the hearts of people who loved us. Decades later, my father still remains real and alive in my memory.

Lessons I Have Learned

- I have learned to accept my life as God's gift, to be cherished and guarded with gratitude. My presence in this world is due to my parents. They did what they could, caring and protecting me, and making my life valuable. They gave me direction using what knowledge, means, and capabilities they had. It was and is my responsibility to accept my genetic endowment and my upbringing, to cherish these things, to preserve them, and to improve them when possible.

- Behind the idea of the personal father whom we know and to whom we relate, lies an innate psychological image that influences the way we experience him. The image functions as a blueprint or barometer of certain features in our daily life. Like a psychological instinct, this image leads us to experience events and people. Simply, as we interact with others, we have preconceived notions of how they should respond to us. We should reflect on where this notion originates.

- Sometimes we end up duplicating our childhood situations in order to get a response resembling our experience with our father or mother. If our father was a benevolent figure as we were growing up, then we seek benevolence in others. On the other hand, if he was a hostile, emotionally detached man, we might seek that type of person for a relationship. Why? One reason, which is a primarily unconscious process, is that it is a familiar interaction. What purpose does it serve? One purpose is to recreate our past in order to correct it or cure our pain about the past.

- The fathering principle must be understood as psychological fathering, as well as biological. Conceivably, a woman can, and in numerous situations does, provide adequate fathering. Articles have been written about this subject, and many psychologists have found that certain mothers fulfill the dual parenting role rather well. Parallel to the scholarly work, there is another indisputable reality, which I believe to be true: our psychologically troubled world is in dire need of psychological fathering.

- Fathering consists of certain qualities that complement mothering and help the child grow into a complete person. These qualities, available also from the mother, are the protecting principles of loving, caring, teaching, and introducing the world to the child. This sort of bonding enhances the child's world. Balanced human growth implies that each parent must contribute a part to make the child complete.

Additional Thoughts

Humans have difficulty in moving out of the comfort of home life and entering the real world. Being "in the world" and being different cause anxiety. We are expected to conform and to be politically correct.

Mass-media daily invades our homes: programs urge us to accept the current vogue to fill our world and to adapt to cultural illusions. Expectations and all-consuming appetites: the nightmarish frenzy in which political maniacs support and unleash terror threats; images of floods, earthquakes, hurricanes, and war—all these suck up our energies and stifle our initiative.

We have an innate instinct for survival. To make our life worthwhile, we need to rediscover the ecstasy of our humanity with its innate godlike strength that helps us to be *in* this world but not *of* this world. This discovery is what could be termed our earthly promised land.

5

Exodus

What we call the beginning is often the end
And to make an end is to make a beginning.
The end is where we start from.
                                        —*T. S. Eliot*

After my twenty-third birthday, I found myself on an ocean liner on its way to the New World. America the beautiful! For me, the journey from Athens to New York was eleven days of anxiety, living among strangers with sad, war-whipped faces—all bound for the promised land. Anticipating the unknown was scary. As the *Marine Shark* furrowed the Atlantic, we were enveloped in sky and sea. By the seventh day there was still no sign of land. In the evening of that day, I sat in the stern in a thick mist, and with a mind as clouded I reminisced about the life I had left behind. The eyes of my soul could clearly see faces of men, women, and children, and hear voices rising into space, hearts throbbing with fear and the echo of despair.

It was September 10, 1944, when I was eighteen when the Nazis finally began their retreat from Greece. Liberation at last came to the young and old of my little village. The Nazi plague was over. I was happy. Early that morning, a solemn parade was held. The villagers marched joyfully, holding a silver cross and a banner depicting the resurrection of Christ, a symbol of liberty. Altar boys carried luminaries, and the Moria Quartet sang the doxology. Papavasile, in colorful vestments, led the procession, and behind him followed a large crowd of exuberant people dressed in Sunday clothes. The procession stopped in front of the town hall. As soon as the priest began to offer a prayer, he was interrupted by thunderous applause.

In wonder, everyone looked toward the balcony of the town hall. Next to the blue Greek flag, a red flag was being raised. It was as large as a blanket and was embroidered with the hammer and sickle, symbols of Soviet Russia. Two speakers arrogantly demanded everyone's attention. One was Seraphim, a teacher to whom the people of Moria had entrusted the education of their children. The other was Anthony, a proponent of communism, a derelict who had never worked a day in his life, although he had the reputation of being an intellectual.

Seraphim was ready with his rehearsed oration. Initially, he praised the supposed liberators and then pronounced his own philosophy:

"God is a myth. What has your faith in God ever done to enhance your life? Communism promises equality, freedom, good life, and abundance. Marx, Lenin, and Stalin are our strong leaders and liberators from the yoke of the plutocrats, the powerful trinity that will make this world a paradise in our time."

Holding the cross and the banner depicting the resurrection of Christ, Papavasile and his altar boys silently walked away from the presence of the rebels, who appeared to be taking over where the Nazis had left off. A small group of aged men and women walked behind the altar boys with bent backs, staring at the ground as though it could reveal what was going to happen next to their homeland. Disturbed, yet curious, I stayed to hear what else my former teacher had to say.

Seraphim's voice echoed across the square, causing my temples to throb.

"Under our leadership, your faith in God is no longer necessary. We promised and now we deliver what all of us needed— freedom from the four-year Nazi occupation, freedom from a god that does not even exist. As your new leaders, we will provide equality, justice, and an abundance of good things. We have your best interests at heart. The curse of exploitation by the plutocrats will no longer threaten you. The first item on our agenda is to assure you that religion is the opium of the masses. It numbs, controls, and gradually kills. It is meant to intimidate you and to make you feel guilty. We want you to be happy citizens and free thinkers. We no longer need churches or priests. The main part of the church building will be used for dances, games, and lectures of interest to you and your children."

While the crowd was applauding, I hurried away to visit Papavasile. I felt anxious and confused and wanted to hear what the good priest had to say about the situation, and what the people would do without a place of worship and without a leader to encourage their belief in God. Was it really true that communism would replace Christianity? It would be a terrible thing to remove God, their great source of consolation, from people's lives.

"Peter, a curse has fallen upon us," Papavasile said sadly. "Dark days are ahead for our homeland. Leave Moria as soon as you can. Go to America where there is freedom, and pray for us. Tell our American friends that the Greek nation will always be their faithful ally."

Communist leaders were determined to destroy even the ruins that the Nazis had left behind. Now the plague came from within our village and spread like fire through the whole island. A civil war broke out, dividing families and demolishing sacred buildings, images, and items. Brothers fought against brothers, and sons rebelled against fathers, causing thousands of deaths in the entire country of Greece.

As the *Marine Shark* plowed the waves, Papavasile's sad voice echoed in my ears and then faded, leaving me with a smile and a sigh. I felt as if I was in Noah's Ark. God had spared our lives. I gazed at the swirling ocean and was awed by the magical wonders and secrets of its depths. The foaming swells shook me into the reality of where I was—on a huge ship bound for the New World. I was embarking on a new beginning that promised more than the little Greek village or communist leaders ever could. Mixed emotions wrestled within, making me feel weak. I trembled like a frightened child. How did I manage to accept such a venture?

How did I get the strength to say goodbye to twenty years of life in Greece? How was I able to leave behind loving relatives and intimate friends? And how was I able to endure the heartbreak of parting from my first love, Eleni? Would I ever be able to fulfill my promise to return to her some day?

With each step we take forward, we leave a step behind, paving our way with "surrenders." We give up some of our deepest and most meaningful relationships. We give up certain cherished places and experiences that we can no longer enjoy. We struggle to adjust to unfamiliar places and establish new relationships. Our past fades as we move on, and our present becomes broader. We let go of ideas that are no longer functional, and we hold onto beliefs that are important to us. Changes, although difficult to accept and implement, bring us closer to maturity and help us discover who we really are. The journey of life continues: an ongoing adaptation. Most of us have difficulty handling the termination of anything. Yet all of us have to deal with endings throughout our lives. It was difficult to leave the land of colors where I had spent my formative years. I buried my dreams, feelings, and thoughts in my heart and traveled across the Atlantic to find my future. It was my new beginning.

Lessons I Have Learned

- Human development, which means *unfolding*, is never static. It continues throughout our whole life, regardless of our circumstances and our location. To find our own place in the world entails leaving behind parental dependency, which was necessary at one time, and taking the risk to travel along untrodden paths. As we progress slowly, we are able to adjust to the next phase of life.

- As the initial excitement and fear of being separated from parental or family dependencies begin to wane, new questions arise, and the emphasis shifts from getting away from a situation to finding and adjusting to a more rewarding situation. Subconsciously, we still seek the promised land.

Additional Thoughts

In view of our survival efforts, we need to rediscover the ecstasy of our humanity with its godlike strength that enables us to be *in* the world, but not *of* this world. We can say with confidence that we are here by God's grace, and that we can fulfill our noble desires by being in harmony with God's will. The question is, Are we willing to put our life in God's hands, and trust that whatever he allows in our life will work for our good?

Not to see immediate results from our efforts can be depressing. There are times when things are difficult and we are tempted to believe that our efforts amount to nothing. That is the time to let faith triumph over doubt, and rest assured that, in God's perfect timing, our efforts will bear fruit. In Saint Paul's words we find comfort and strength: "Let us not become weary in doing good, for in proper time we will reap a harvest if we do not give up" (Gal 6:9).

PART TWO
Choosing

6

Choices of the Heart

*The wise person looks beneath the surface and chooses what
is real.*   —T. S. Eliot

June 21, 1946, marked a new chapter in my life. I arrived at
Uncle Nick's house in Philadelphia, Pennsylvania. He was my
father's brother, "a giant of knowledge and wealth," according to
my father. Uncle Nick had established himself in America in
1905. My father had convinced me that Uncle Nick would be my
savior, my guardian, and the overseer of my education.

Uncle Nick received me joyfully. He was a swarthy man, tall
like my father, and austere looking. We sat down to our first meal
together. He paused to teach me table etiquette, and that was
where I learned to handle silverware. Thus far in my life, my eating utensils had consisted of a fork and a spoon. Using a fork
and a knife at the same time did not come easily to me. While
Uncle Nick drank his beer and munched on a cracker spread
with Limburger cheese, he kept an eye on my manners. He offered
me a Coke.

"America! America!" he said. "Land of opportunity! A great
country! You don't know how lucky you are! You can even
become the president of the United States, if you want. But I
would not be satisfied even if you did become president. I want
you to be more than a president."

A president? I had no notion of what he was trying to tell me.
I kept staring at him without blinking, trying to read his mind. I
was but a village boy, an olive picker. At this point I was not able

47

to speak a word of English, and yet he expected me to be more than a president of a nation! I smiled nervously at the very idea.

"You are my brother's son. I have high expectations for you," he said, and as he kept talking, I realized that my uncle wallowed in megalomania. He considered himself an authority on many aspects of life—socioeconomic, political, religious, philosophical—and he was taking it upon himself to plan my future, although he did not even know what sort of person I was. "Remember who you are. You and I come from noble ancestors: Socrates, Plato, Aristotle, Alexander the Great." I had some elementary knowledge of these names, but what did they have to do with me, a village boy who aspired to get a job and save enough money for a return trip to be with my friends and with Eleni to share our life together?

Two weeks later, my uncle and I walked through the city of Philadelphia on our way to Temple University. I was in awe of what I saw and I felt ecstatic with my new surroundings. The flow of straight streets and avenues, the symmetry of trees planted along sidewalks, the majesty of the buildings—what a fantastic sight! This mythical elegance was the product of what the New World called industrial civilization. This is it—the promised land! This was my birthplace, the city where I had spent the first three years of my life. Why did my father leave this earthly paradise and take me to a little Greek island? I was making a transition from yesterday's agony to today's ecstasy.

Uncle Nick and I arrived at the gate of the university. I was dumbfounded at the size of the buildings and the swarms of young and old moving to and fro, carrying books, and speaking a language foreign to my ears. My heart pounded rapidly as all the yesterdays began to haunt my soul. I felt homesick, and my mind traveled back to my little village with its narrow streets and whitewashed houses where every stone had been put in place by human hands, and where people were bound together by invisible ties—*memories sweeter than honey*. Philadelphia was another world of sights, sounds, and smells; it was a world where swarms of well-fed and well-dressed people bustled about their business.

· As we entered the office of the registrar, we were welcomed with smiles and amenities. My uncle introduced me to several important people. With a grin on his face, he rambled on and periodically turned to me. I shrugged my shoulders. I did not understand a word of what was said, but I assumed it was about my higher education. After our brief encounter with school authorities, without explaining to me what had transpired, Uncle Nick told me that the school expected me to become fluent in the English language before being accepted for premedical studies.

"You will make a fine doctor, and I will be a proud uncle."

"A doooctoor!" I exclaimed in amazement. Yesterday I was to become more than a president; today I was to become a doctor. What gave him such an idea? What made him think he had the right to decide what I was going to be? Medicine? A doctor? The thought had never crossed my mind. As far as I was concerned, my career decision would be exclusively mine. Yet I decided that the time was not appropriate to confront my uncle. I realized that my stay at his house would be short. I had come to this great country to enjoy freedom, only to find myself under this man's domination. I needed a plan of escape.

On each side of the corridor leading to the university offices were columns that served as pedestals for the busts of important historical personalities. As we were leaving, Uncle Nick pointed to *our ancestors*. I recognized the names and was duly impressed. However, more interesting to me was a statue of the Sphinx. Engraved in the Greek language on the plaque below was the riddle:

What walks on four feet in the morning,
two feet at noon,
and three feet in the evening?

I had come across the riddle of the Sphinx in high school. It was humorous, but I never gave it much thought then. That day, the riddle was no longer a mere test of wit. Walking on four feet symbolized infancy, a state of dependency. Walking on two at noon implied adult years. Walking on three referred to old age when a person needed a cane for support. Proud to read the Greek inscription, I understood the valuable lesson of wisdom it imparted to me. It was time for me to *stand* in the world on my own two feet and make my own decisions. The time had come for me to lead a true adult life, to discover who I was and what life was all about. What was it that lay behind the world's facade, animating it, ordering it in a particular direction? I wanted to find out.

My return to America offered me a special kind of opportunity to break with the social condition that had carried me thus far and to do something really new and different. Within myself was an urge, a force, a deep prompting of the spirit, pushing me to pursue a life that made sense to me. My aim was to live a life of simplicity; to be socially useful, ethical and productive; and to earn enough money to return to the island of Lesvos where I had experienced my first love. How could I ever explain my thoughts to Uncle Nick who, in forty years, had not once visited his native land?

―――― Ꮿ Ꮿ ――――

From childhood, I had been fascinated with the church. I wanted to become a priest. The priesthood seemed to be my destination.

"A priest? What's wrong with you?" Uncle Nick said. "You're turning your back on a promising future in the world of medicine. I took you to one of the finest universities in America! It doesn't make sense at all."

"Uncle Nick, I've always wanted to become a priest," I said, noticing disappointment in his face. "That's what I really want to be."

The seminary was my choice and my responsibility. It also became part of my definition. My proclivities were toward religious pageantry and joyful variations of Byzantine music and chant. Because I had been an olive picker and still had my village manners, the seminary seemed like a place for honing me, removing my impurities, polishing my rough spots. I would emerge glossy and shiny from the Holy Cross Greek Orthodox Seminary, like a car completed on the assembly line. As a priest, I would serve my church in any way I could, give direction to people's lives, educate them about a godly life, save their souls, and perform my duties with absolute devotion and forthrightness.

I faithfully went through theological training, disciplined fasting and prayer, scholarly biblical studies, and daily rituals amid clouds of smoke from incense. All this brought me to the end of the priest production-line. I completed the five-year course of intense studies in three. As the time of my ordination approached, the yearning to go out into the world and bear witness of what I had learned increased. I was ready, but was I? The ecclesiastical authorities dictated, *You must find a wife.*

Greek Orthodox priests must be married *before* their ordination, if they are to marry at all. They may not marry *after* their ordination. So if a future priest does not feel called to celibacy, he has to marry beforehand. This was the rule and it had to be obeyed. The chosen woman has to be modest and dedicated to the church; she must be above reproach in manners and dress; she must be unconditionally devoted to her priest-husband; she has to be or to have the likeliness of being a good mother; and she has to be an exemplary wife, a role model in the parish.

How can any male decide in his early twenties who can be his mate for a lifetime? I was fresh out of the seminary, and since leaving Lesvos, I had seldom been alone with a female. It was a challenge to go in search of the ideal *presvytera,* a priest's wife. In spite of the hormonal drive, the thought of marriage caused me panic, so I decided to continue my education and postpone the decision.

My seminary training emphasized theology, church history, and dogmatics. These were necessary courses to lay a strong foundation for an authentic priesthood. But there were no courses to teach us how to channel the energy and vitality that exist in every parish in a spiritual direction. Also, there were no courses that taught family dynamics or what it means to be a married person.

Several of my classmates felt a need to be more spiritual. We wanted our studies to lead us into an ever-growing communion with God, with each other, and with our fellow human beings. Rituals and symbols were impressive, but we wished for something more. That *something* caused anxiety in our young, naive minds. How were we to offer the rich mystical traditions of Christianity, which the major church personalities propagated, as a source of "the newness of life" in the midst of a materialistic civilization?

Isn't this also our reality today? Many people experience increasing anxiety and daily stress. Not finding relief anywhere in their present life or in material possessions, they search for a new life. The church can be effective in our lives only when every advice given and every message offered come from hearts that understand and love Christ intimately.

My search led me to pursue further studies at Philadelphia Divinity School and Princeton Theological Seminary. It was an experience in pastoral psychology—the study of the soul. I visualized that a synthesis of psychology and theology could bring "new life" into our society, as promised by Christ. As an instrument of God's grace, I had to offer practical steps to his people: how to find freedom of the spirit, a life of joy and peace that the world could not give. In developing a deeper faith and belief in who Christ really was—God in human flesh—I gained a better understanding of the reason why God chose to reveal himself in human form. His incarnation and involvement with people as a man gave evidence of his unconditional love and concern for a faltering humanity. He chose to become one of us that we might learn to emulate his life. When I was ordained, compassion, forgiveness, love, and relief from suffering were my major objectives to be pursued in my ministry, as well as passing on skills for Christian living.

Three years later, I grappled once again with the question of marriage. As a graduate with a master's degree in theology, I was eager to enter the real world and offer my services as a priest. Yet, there was one thing missing: I had no prospect for a wife. To divert the attention of the hierarchy, who were adamant about my getting married before being ordained, I thought I could start a vigorous fund-raising drive for our seminary in Brookline, Massachusetts. With such an important activity, I could still delay marriage for at least another year, claiming that I was still in search of a wife.

I truly felt profound gratitude toward the school that educated me, and our seminary needed funds for survival. So I returned to Philadelphia, the city of my birth, and knocked on doors, asking for donations. Many people responded favorably and gave handsome donations or made an annual pledge or requested time to think about it. During my contact with individuals, families, and business personnel, I met a young woman who was a radio announcer. There was an attractive glow in her appearance, her chestnut hair was combed to perfection, she was modestly dressed, she had on no makeup, and she had a strong handshake. Her name was Mary. She received me graciously and invited me to speak on her radio program. Excited by her offer, I accepted the invitation. She gave me the address, and we met at WKDN radio station in Camden, New Jersey, the following Sunday.

The meeting was cordial. Mary tested my voice and explained to me the mechanics of the radio program. She noticed I was nervous, and she gently demonstrated how to approach the microphones: "Nothing to it. Relax and talk to the mike as you would talk to a friend." At 2:00 p.m. she started the program with enthusiasm and a jovial voice, informing the audience that she was pleased to welcome a special guest. She looked at me, blushed, and announced the current events.

My heart palpitated with mixed emotions. *Am I the special guest? Will my prepared speech appeal to her audience? Will it appeal to her?* I totally forgot what I was about to say. With blurred vision, I looked at my manuscript, but my blood kept rising to my head. More nervous than ever, I saw her gesturing to me to come and sit next to her in front of the microphone.

At 2:15 p.m., with extraordinary charm she announced my name. I was the *special guest,* a theologian and future priest. She turned the microphone toward me and nodded for me to start. I took a deep breath and rolled my tongue around my dry mouth. It is moments like this that God's grace comes to our assistance, provided our intentions are good. Out of the corner of my eye, I saw Mary shaking her head and smiling. Obviously she approved of my message, and I felt more confident. As soon as I had finished my presentation, the phones began to ring off the hook. Listeners called the station, eager to make a donation. Mary answered with excitement, acknowledging the names of the donors and tabulating the amounts donated. By the end of the program, the sum had risen to over three thousand dollars, not a small amount for the early fifties, and the phones kept on ringing. More donations came through, and we sat in the lounge to chat. She wanted to know about the seminary. Then her questions took a different direction.

"What made you decide to become a priest?" she asked.

I told her that, since childhood, I was fascinated with the church, and as I grew older, my desire to become a priest became stronger.

"Isn't a priest's life somewhat restricted?"

"To some extent."

"Does the church permit you to get married and have children?"

"Of course! Before my ordination I have to get married."

"You must have found someone who wants to be a priest's wife."

"Not yet," I said. I wondered if *she* would like to be a priest's wife.

"I would not want to be a priest's wife," she said. "Nothing personal, but I see that life as being too conservative, too much under the public eye."

A week later, she called to tell me that more donations had come in, and if I wanted to make another presentation on WKDN, I would be more than welcome. I thanked her for the offer and said that I would like to give it some thought. The topic then changed:

"Why do you want to become a priest? You could be a professor. Then you could really enjoy life."

I tried to explain to her that I visualized a great future in the church and I was happy with my decision. Obviously, she liked me and found reasons to call me. During these calls, we discovered many similarities in our background. We were both born in America but we grew up in Greece and had lived there during World War II. Further, we found out that we were both motherless, had both traveled to Greece on the ship the *Edison* in 1929, and had both returned to America in 1946.

During these phone dialogues, I perceived the similarities in our background, and I believed they were not coincidental. The more we talked about our lives, the more I told myself that probably it was God's way of pointing her out as my mate. The idea of returning to Greece to marry Eleni gradually faded; in fact, she had married the son of a dentist, so I was now free and happy that I had met another woman who could be my wife. In spite of her initial resistance to the thought of being a priest's wife, Mary became regular in her church attendance. When I preached a sermon, she managed to find a seat in the front pew. One Sunday, she invited me to her house to meet her father and brother. It was a pleasant visit, and I felt welcome.

As I was leaving, she escorted me to the door, and in a soft voice, she said, "I'm curious. Is a priest's wife permitted to dance?"

"Of course! She is not the priest," I said, looking her straight in the eye.

"I love to dance," she said and lowered her eyes.

Reciprocal phone calls followed, and on Sundays after church her brother joined us for lunch. Months later, I asked her if she would consider becoming my wife, knowing that my decision to become a priest was irrevocable. She said yes with overwhelming enthusiasm. Two sacraments, holy matrimony and holy orders, took place within the same year.

On June 8, 1952, we were married, and on December 9, 1952, I was ordained. The following Sunday, I took up a position serving a parish in Newark, New Jersey. The following year we were blessed with the birth of a little girl named Mercene. Two years later, we had an additional blessing: my son Michael was born. In church, I was the spiritual father of many people, but at home I was the natural father of two beautiful children, a family man. Married life and priestly career were put into full action by my twenty-eighth year of life. It was exciting to be a spiritual leader, yet it became increasingly difficult to give equal attention to both church and family.

Parish life was awesome and demanding. I sensed the need to be loving and humble enough to accept guidance from on high. Preaching the Gospel and eloquent sermons, administering the sacraments, and celebrating religious services were the visible tasks that any priest could perform. I was determined to make my parish a community of love and cooperation, reaching beyond the boundaries of the church building. My enthusiasm consumed time and energy, and left me little time for family life. The needs of the parishioners came first. I wanted my people to experience the joy of helping the less fortunate, to engage in the human struggle, and to rediscover the true meaning of Christian life. I often spoke of the finitude of this world, basing my thoughts on the words of Saint Paul that we truly have no city in which to stay, we must seek our heavenly one (Heb 13:14). Then I would add a personal comment, that our material accumulations and diligent efforts to succeed in this life ultimately mean very little.

Lessons I Have Learned

- Developing or establishing a new identity, distinct from others, is a calculated process that requires time and honesty. Who we are, and how we would like to design our personal life, are issues that require serious thought and responsible action. Failing to follow the process leaves us insecure and unsure of who we are and where we are heading.

- Entering the adult world can be intimidating. It takes acceptance of who we are, and awareness of who others are, in order to interact with them and eventually forge new interpersonal relationships. "Make haste slowly" is a good axiom to keep in mind as we experiment with situations with an eye to making commitments.

- Decisions are personal issues. Sometimes they are made a long time before they are implemented. Each decision we make has its own consequences that affect the decision-makers and their immediate surroundings. Therefore, decisions require responsibility. Realistic thinking, patience, and persistence pave the way for realization of good plans.

- Sometimes we discover what we really want in life, and then we experience that *Ah-ha!* feeling of elation. At other times, circumstances change our direction, leaving us with limited choices. Accepting what we have not chosen, although difficult, often offers new opportunities.

Additional Thoughts

Some people design for themselves a manageable world; they throw themselves into action uncritically, unthinkingly. They accept cultural programming, turning their head to where they are supposed to look. They use all kinds of techniques—known as character defenses; they learn to embed themselves in other powers or ideals, both of concrete persons and of things and cultural commands. The result is that they come to exist in the imagined infallibility of the world around them.

—Ernest Becker

7

Love One Another

Each man is an island unto himself, and the bridges that lead to other people have been destroyed by conflicts of race, sex, and self-interest. —Robert D. Spector

On my forty-second birthday, I thought about the above quotation. *A grim picture of all times,* I thought. I was a priest, so building bridges among people was a major part of my ministry. In spite of the pessimism of the quotation, I had to do my part to connect people in a spirit of love, charity, and cooperation.

The potential, the ability of each one of us to reach out and touch another human, is where we begin. A smile, accompanied by a handshake and a good word, can accomplish a great deal in our interaction with others. There is no need to be gloomy, grouchy, and greedy; there is no need to add to the population of egocentric and negative people. However, there is also no need to be angry or to pass judgment on such people; we do not really know their circumstances, nor do we know why they feel the way they do. Maybe their self-image is suffering. They may be lacking confidence in themselves because of an earlier emotional deprivation. What part should we play in their lives? We could ignore them; we could isolate ourselves and become "islands"; or we could see them as creatures of God, as fellow-travelers in the journey of life. It does not require much effort to say "Hello! How are you?" Or simply to offer a smile. We may be surprised when we discover that interesting people and beautiful souls are among us.

In my daily walk, I used to cross paths with a man who was a vigorous jogger. I always said, "Good morning," although he never responded. He did not even look at me. I often thought of ignoring him, but that did not sit well with me. I increased my greeting: "Good morning. It's a beautiful day!" Oblivious of me, he jogged past. Now, I had a choice: I could do what he did— move on and mind my business, or I could continue to pay attention to his presence.

One day, instead of my verbal greeting, I waved at him. He smiled and waved back. It was a good sign. I said, "You are really a good jogger." As he continued on his path, he called over his shoulder, "Thank you." The following week I introduced myself, and he replied, "I'm Joe. I live on Wood Valley Road." "Then we're neighbors," I said. "I live a block away from you." That happened a few years ago, and now Joe and I usually stop every morning, exchange a friendly greeting, and chat for a few minutes. Some people avoid talking to us because they are afraid we may discover who they are. If *they* do not like who they are, the thought that we may reject them frightens them off. This may be true about anyone.

In our times, threatened by the unfamiliar or the unknown— terrorist warnings, law-and-order problems, mistrust of government officials, financial insecurity, loss of retirement savings, fear of walking the streets at night—we tend to tear down the bridges and retreat behind the walls and security of our homes. We become little islands. Each day, as we view the six o'clock news on television or read the newspapers, depressing feelings enter our inner world where crime, murder, violence, and war roll around in our head. Hundreds are killed, thousands do not have enough to eat, children are neglected, and there appears to be no education and no plan for a better tomorrow. Is this what life is all about?

Unresolved issues still left me unsettled. My enthusiasm over my priestly identity—being called *Father*, a title bestowed upon me at my ordination several years earlier—slowly subsided. I began to see what Christ meant when he said, "My Kingdom is not from this world" (John 18:36). Did I understand what he meant? Hardly! He spoke of a different life, a spiritual dimension of existence. How could I convey a sense of spirituality in a materially saturated world? My job description included, besides the spiritual welfare of the congregation, responsibility for its financial survival, which meant events such as festivals, picnics, athletic activities, and raffle tickets. I had to be a good fundraiser! The last thing I ever wanted to do was to go from door to door soliciting money or planning social events to produce revenue. I had done all that when I was young and naive. That was not my perception of being a priest. The training at the seminary omitted such a course.

To be married to the church "for better, for worse, for richer, for poorer, till death do us part" was the commitment I had made. I could not back out of it or stubbornly jump ahead and do what my heart dictated. Trying to educate the parish about the principles of Christianity, charity, compassion, love for one another, and forgiveness was like swimming against the current. As I described my frustrations to my superior, the local bishop, he suggested sacrifice, humility, patience, and prayer. Calmly, he sanctioned lay leadership and sacrifice of personal interests. He lived in his own comfortable doubt about God's will with regard to poverty and pain, and the complacency of the rich and famous. "God has the best plans in mind for all people." How could the bishop still speak with authority about social justice, divine providence, and trust in God's plan?

While these questions lingered in my mind, I could not challenge the bishop for answers. Who was I to judge the hierarchical authority? I had to pull back and examine my thoughts; they were an arrogant attempt to satisfy my ego and ignore the bishop's position. If I were to serve people as a priest, I had to leave judgments in God's hands and seek to understand what God desired of me. As important as it seemed to love, obey, please, and worship God, what I needed was to be humble and to have genuine concern for others. I realized that in my own subtle ways I was ambitious and proud. I loved success, cherished accomplishments, tried to make an impression on others, sought approval, and looked for praise. In the process, I ignored the fact that I was simply a laborer in God's own vineyard. Intense was the temptation to receive credit, to be recognized, to put God aside, and to exalt myself. To a great extent, this is the problem we all face:

Each one of us wants to feel important. Yet we forget the truth, that in God's eyes, all of us are important. As the Bible claims, we are the *very special* products of his love. He brought us to life, endowed in his image and likeness. That means we are his co-creators, and we have an immortal soul. He has given us a beautiful world to enjoy. So why do we spoil our lives and the lives of others around us with our bad behavior, apathy, arrogance, false ego, gluttony, greed, and selfishness?

To avoid falling into the dangerous trap of pride, I needed to discern between positive pride—good feelings of doing something worthwhile in the eyes of God—and negative pride—pursuing projects for personal glory, and failing to acknowledge God, the Giver of all Blessings. I had to minimize my impact upon people, cease trying to impress them, and realize the work of the Holy Spirit through me. I was simply an instrument in God's hands. That is what we all are: God's tools used by his power to pursue our salvation, well-being, and happiness on earth so that we may attain the glory of his reward once our earthly life comes to an end.

In spite of my theological education, it took a long time to see myself as an instrument of God. What I needed was a large dose of humility and spiritual maturity. I had to learn to live with compassion. The Lord was very clear when he said, "I did not come to be served, I came to serve." Humble behavior permeated his entire ministry. During the last hours before his crucifixion, he washed the feet of his disciples. Was that a sign of weakness? Or was it the ultimate example of humility? His birth in a stable, his mortal presence among people, his final entrance into Jerusalem—not riding in a chariot or on a horse as a king, but on a simple donkey—and his tragic death on the Hill of Golgotha: in all these, we see a life of utmost humility.

As Christians, we are given a message worthy of considering: to become aware of the Lord's presence in our life. He directs us away from personal pride and desire of possessions, and points to a simple way of living where there is peace and contentment. It is through simplicity that our hearts become tender to the needs of the poor. An old saying claims: "The one whose stomach is always full can never understand how a hungry person feels."

Granted, living in a competitive, me-first society and wanting to climb higher and higher up the ladder of success, it is difficult to be humble. Humility may be seen as a sign of weakness. We may lose out and be left behind in the corporate world, while others gain success. Christ's message is reassuring: *The one who is humble shall be raised high.* When we choose to live the Christian life, there is one fact on which we can absolutely rely: God has a specific plan and purpose for each one of us. Instead of striving for higher positions or envying other people's apparent success, we can be grateful for our present position and each day strive to do the best we can, experiencing the joy of daily living within God's will, which guarantees peace. God's love and immeasurable mercy are his gifts to us. It is our choice to accept these gifts gratefully or to ignore their existence.

As the hierarchy managed to avoid everything taught by Christ, local churches also evaded the unmistakable concerns of the Gospel with regard to poverty and violence, the destructive influence of our materially saturated society, and the indifference of arrogant governments and affluent Christians.

I could not abide the hierarchical mentality that tended to make God—and other people, for that matter—into who they wanted him to be and needed him to be. I was under the impression that it was the role of the priest to keep his people free for God. But at the same time, it was the priest's responsibility to keep God free for people. Of course, I could not interpret God the way I perceived Divinity myself, either. Can any human, however theologically educated he or she is, define God? The only human knowledge we could have about God is the personality of Jesus Christ, who is God in human flesh.

For a long time, I experienced a sense of personal loneliness, even when I was among gatherings of people who attended church or religious rituals. The best way I was able to diffuse that lonely feeling was to write textbooks for religious education classes. I had strong faith in the potential of young people whose hearts and minds were still pure and receptive.

Years later, as a therapist, I realized that loneliness is one of the universal sources of troubled souls who seek to be comforted. An effective way to emerge from the labyrinth of loneliness that crushes many people is the challenge to see the reality of life, face its ramifications, and attempt to make it more humane and more simple. There is joy and peace in simple things.

Of course, most of us realize the influence of the advertising industry with its artificial and deceptive messages, telling us how we can escape the malady of loneliness. All we need is a credit card to buy ourselves anything in sight—electronic devices, cellular phones, gadgets, luxuries, possessions, and better and bigger belongings. Clever merchants claim to know what we need.

The realization that no other person can completely think, feel, or act the way we do offers us the freedom of choice. My choice surfaced gradually. I had to be responsible for my personal life. My life as a priest was already planned by Jesus Christ, God in human flesh, who had chosen a handful of dedicated disciples and changed the course of human history. What a great honor and responsibility it was for me to stand with his disciples and to bring the good news, the immortal teachings of Christ among his people!

As difficult as it seemed, I had to let God be a God who is greater than our theological knowledge, greater than our own projections. Before I conveyed any authentic knowledge about God to my congregation, I needed to learn who I was, my own reality of being human.

A God who favors certain people and ignores others, allowing tragedies to occur, was not acceptable to me. God created us after his image and likeness: in no way can we make God after our human image and likeness.

It was Jesus Christ and the apostle Paul who removed the boundaries and spoke emphatically about a God of love and reconciliation. When I read about the earthly life of Jesus and thought of his unconditional love, healing ministry, compassion, and forgiveness, when I thought about how responsibly he related to all people, I felt inspired. At the same time, I recognized my ineptness, not simply to imitate him, but to implement his teachings.

How could I ever discuss or share these concerns, personal dilemmas, with any of my superiors? I guarded myself against being antagonistic to my ministry, and I guarded myself from being threatened with suspension. I had a wife and children who needed my support, and the church provided my only income. Shy by nature, I kept my thoughts to myself, realizing that at times even noble ambitions cannot be fulfilled. What was I to do? Feel sorry for myself? Our ancestors provided the answer: Get deeper into yourself and learn from yourself what you must do. The choice was evident. You must do what your soul dictates and not expect approval or support.

St. Basil, a fourth-century church father, encapsulated the ministry of the church and the mission of every Christian in these words:

> According to the abundance of Your mercy, fill our life with good things; preserve our families in peace and harmony; nurture the infants, instruct the youth, embrace and support the elderly, comfort the discouraged, bring back closer to You those who have gone astray. Free those who are possessed by negative or evil thoughts. Sail with those at sea, be a companion with those who travel, defend the widows, protect the orphans, free the prisoners, and heal the sick and suffering.
>
> Remember those who love us and those who hate us, and forgive those who reject us. Lord, extend your mercy to the helpless, give hope to the hopeless, for You are the Father of all, the Healer of all ailments, the Savior of our bodies and souls who knows the name and the age of each one of us, and You know our needs even from our mother's womb.
>
> —A prayer from St. Basil's Liturgy, AD 330–79

These words place us in the hands of God. We trust God and we ask him to be in control of our lives. We surrender slowly to his loving guidance. Once we let God be present in our life, then we extend his loving care to others by kindness, charity, and good attitude.

One may say, "Well, this is what the church *should* do." Wonderful! But who is the church? You and I are the church. As

Saint Paul puts it, "You are the body of Christ and individually members of it" (1 Cor 12:27–28). The Church consists of baptized Christians who believe in Christ and practice his teachings. When we become part of this mission, each one of us does whatever is possible—within his or her reality—for the good of others. "There are varieties of gifts, but the same Spirit," Saint Paul emphasizes, "and there are varieties of services, but the same Lord; and there are varieties of activities, but it is the same God who activates all of them in everyone" (1 Cor 12:4–7). "Strive for the greater gifts. And I will show you a still more excellent way" (1 Cor 12:31). A proper way to being open to whatever gift we have within us is to avoid being negative, and to stop blaming or judging others. Wow! Don't you feel a tinge of joy already in taking that first step, and with minimum hesitation reaching out and touching someone's life?

During this period I learned to love many things about life. I loved that which some people did not care about, and yet, at times, I loathed aspects of life that people loved. I loved to reach out and help people in need. I chose to visit hospitals, where I spent time with terminally ill patients. It was difficult to make progress for the church. For example, when I suggested to our parish leaders a project to help our overseas missions, there were subtle resistances. I asked certain well-to-do parishioners to donate money for a child who needed open-heart surgery. The parish president said, "Our own community has many financial needs. Missionary work is a project for charities."

People are the architects of their lives; they have freedom of choice to design their lives as they please. Perhaps they should not deprive themselves of anything they desire. I find that hard to stomach. But is it that difficult to extend a benevolent hand and help others who are in dire need of food, clothing, or medicine?

All humans are challenged with the question: *As one person with little resources at my disposal, what can I possibly do? I can scarcely make ends meet.* The answer lies with each individual. In spite of our circumstances, there is something each one of us can do. No matter how poor in money or in talent or in position we are, there is a gift that each one of us can give. Any person with a normal nature can extend tenderness, love, affection, and sympathy.

The child, the teenager, the lover, the wife, the husband, the elderly, the weak, the oppressed, and even the criminal—they all could use a kind word or an expression of compassion, and through it they would certainly note a tremendous change in their lives.

Wisdom from Confucius brings this chapter to a close:

> If there is righteousness in the heart, there will be
> beauty in the character.
> If there is beauty in the character, there will be harmony in the home.
> If there is harmony in the home, there will be order in
> the nation.
> If there is order in each nation, there will be peace in
> the world.

Lessons I Have Learned

- Ideals are like the stars. We aspire to reach them, but we cannot. It is better to be realistic and not beat ourselves with delusions. Superman and superwoman are illusions meant to excite our senses and lead us into a fantasy world. Can we really live an exciting, successful, wealthy superlife as proclaimed in magazines and television?

- We admire the rich and famous, movie celebrities, accomplished athletes, authors, and artists—they all appear glamorous and happy. Yet, do we know what their real lives are like? Do we know how they feel off the stage? Legendary characters who to us seem so noble rarely have the individual qualities that mass media creatively glorifies.

- When we compare ourselves with others, usually we seek individuals who seem to excel; they are more gifted, more talented, more of everything. We wish to be like others who look great—at least, great in our perception. Then we feel our spirits lagging because we don't even come close to them. We can be only who we are, and that's a blessing.

- As we travel down life's highway, we can remind ourselves that we are who we are, worthy human beings, and we can do good things for ourselves and for others. If people in our path treat us badly or try to tear us down or block our growth with negative thoughts, we need to understand that these people project onto us their own mental conditions. At best, we can avoid them, for they can disturb our life.

- When we associate with negative people—whether they are needy friends, overbearing parents, demanding bosses, stubborn spouses, or crazy relatives—they can be poisonous playmates. We don't need to adopt or approve their lifestyle so they can love us. When we design or redesign our life, we need nobody's approval.

- As well-rounded as we can be, we are still human with complex and contradictory attitudes. Our lives tend to be complicated, like a jig-saw puzzle, but we can figure out where the pieces go, and we can fit them carefully together where they belong. We have the chance to move on, living and doing whatever good our hearts dictate.

Additional Thoughts

The whole purpose of the church was founded on philanthropy. "Love one another as I have loved you," said Jesus. "You are my friends if you do what I command you" (John 15:12–14). "God is love, and those who abide in love abide in God, and God abides in them" (1 John 4:16).

To understand the mysteries of God and his creation cannot be done by our intellect alone. It requires faith, getting to know who we really are, accepting and refining our own personalities, and responding to others with compassion and love. We understand the familiar saying, "Charity begins at home." There is no reason it should not travel from home to lands abroad. In our prosperous country, where we enjoy an abundance of goods, we could easily extend a helping hand to the less fortunate, the hungry, and homeless. We are capable of expanding the circle of our charity and sympathy to encompass others in need.

There is no philanthropy equal to that which the gospel plants in the human heart. It turns the severest sacrifices for Christ and humanity into pleasures and aspirations that grow only in the garden of love.

8

Wants and Needs

Genuine religion leads us beyond egocentric attitudes and helps us to see who we really are, and to appropriate the divine potential with us. From God's point of view we have the freedom to be ordinary—the choices we make indicate where we would like to be. —Richard Rohr

With the passing of another birthday, the sudden realization that I was now middle-aged shook me. With half of my life lived, I felt it was imperative to answer three familiar questions I had pondered for many years: *Who am I? What have I accomplished or learned thus far? Where am I going?* Facing reality is a scary business. It's no wonder that the word *reality* is not popular. As T. S. Eliot said, "Human beings cannot bear very much reality."

Middle years! At that time, I thought I had matured and could distinguish reality from nonreality. I could not tolerate superficial living. I could not understand how people could submit themselves to the idols of materialism and greed; nor could I understand why they were so easily influenced by the shrewd seduction of advertising. My spirit became restless. I wanted to raise my voice and tell people how I felt. In sharing my feelings with an older colleague, he smiled and pointed to his bald head. He said, "Early in my life I had thick wavy hair like yours, but I lost it over the years, trying to change people. People don't change. The best you can hope for is that they will mature." The message was clear. In spite of my perceptions of the materially saturated environment, I knew I had choices. I needed to grow and be more of a person myself.

For four years during World War II, when the Nazis occupied Greece, including my little island of Lesvos, hundreds of the islanders died of starvation and human cruelty. I was there. I witnessed the death of many children. I could not understand why children died; I thought death came only to the elderly. Later, as a priest of the Greek Orthodox Cathedral in Los Angeles, I had to perform funerals of young children, and my mission was to console parents grieving over one of the most painful losses in life. In my naive manner, I entitled death with sweet expressions: *Death is the gateway to paradise....Death takes children away to protect them from a world of evil and corruption....God wants to have innocent children in his kingdom.*

At times, when anxiety would dry my tongue and words would not come to my lips, I wondered what God would say about the death of children: *I want only children in my kingdom. I like children because my image has not yet been tarnished in them. They are new, pure, without a blot or smear. I like them because they are still growing; they are still improving. They make mistakes as they grow, but they don't mean any harm. In my heaven, there will be children, and only adults with children's hearts, for I know nothing more beautiful than the pure eyes of a child. I, your God, live in children, and it is I who look out through their eyes. When pure eyes meet yours, it is I who smile at you through those innocent eyes. When death occurs, I am with you to bring back to life the child in you.*

As I recollect these words today, I think they were probably of little comfort to those parents. No words of wisdom or wise counsel can bring much solace to a suffering soul. I believe that grieving parents appreciate even the silent presence of a good friend. However, if we could possibly look at life through God's eyes, we would see it as innumerable tokens of the Creator's love wanting his creatures to be loving. God brought us into the world, not to walk through it with lowered eyes, but to search for him through things, events, and people, and through his wonderful creation of the universe.

Realizing that life and death walk hand in hand, I felt profound longing to share my love and compassion with those who

70

had loved and suffered. Each time I turned to the right or left, the opportunity seemed to be ever-present.

At that time, I had a chance to visit my aging parents, who were still settled in Greece on the island of Lesvos. While there, Theodore Skinas, the director of an orphanage, approached me and asked if I could help his boys. He said, "We have 160 boys. We feed them, educate them, teach them a trade, and help them to become good citizens." I asked him what kind of help he thought I could offer.

"You live in America-a-a, very rich country," he said with a gracious smile. "Perhaps you could find one or two wealthy people to...you know..." He paused.

"What do you need?"

"Well, for starters, we don't have a refrigerator or a freezer to store food that local people donate. I need help to buy fabric to make new uniforms for my children." He always referred to the orphans as *his children*. "The Holy Days of Christmas and the New Year will be here in another month, and I want my children to have something new to wear."

It was a Saturday in November when I decided to visit the orphanage. Conditions were not ideal. The building was old, although elegant looking on the outside. The dormitories were large, each holding more than thirty beds. The damp walls were peeling. The place appeared clean and all the beds were neatly made, but the entire edifice needed to be refurbished. The wooden floors were bare; one or two faded pictures of war heroes decorated the walls. In certain rooms, teachers taught classes in carpentry, furniture-making, shoemaking, and tailoring.

Mr. Skinas took me on a tour of part of the facility. Each time we entered a room, the boys stood and bowed. Mr. Skinas asked the trainees to sit down, and introduced me as a guest from America. Beautiful swarthy faces with crew cuts and big dark brown eyes looked at us respectfully. Their clothes were in tatters and their sandals had seen better days. "Oh! America!" The boys whispered and smiled. I wondered what thoughts lay behind their innocent exclamations.

By the time we had covered all areas, a loud bell rang. Work stopped, and the boys emerged from their rooms and headed toward the dining room. Tactfully, everyone took his place. Mr. Skinas invited me to join him and the personnel for lunch. We sat at the head table. Everyone stood for grace, which was offered by one of the older boys. The whole meal consisted of a dish of fried potatoes for each boy, a slice of dark bread, and an apple; glasses of water were available at the table, but juice and milk were not part of the diet. The boys ate silently, and their eyes kept wandering to the VIPs at the head table.

The potatoes, fried in pure olive oil, were delicious; dessert and salad were not on the menu. My mind played an instant picture of American children back home, sitting around the table, eating a variety of nourishing food. How much these orphans would enjoy an American Sunday dinner complete with a dessert! Why should our American children have so much and these children have so little? The thought saddened me. I drank the lukewarm water. Mr. Skinas noticed my grimace and said, "Our water is not cold. That's why we need a refrigerator in this place. At least my children should have cold drinking water, especially during summer." Who would have thought such an institution would be lacking in what we consider the ordinary things of life?

At the end of the meal, the tables were cleared instantly. The boys walked out of the building and stood in single file on a soccer field. An instructor brought out a bike, and the first boy in line took a ride around the field, and when his turn was over, he joined the end of the line to wait for a second turn. The second in line took his turn, and so the pattern continued. I could not believe what I saw.

It was beyond my imagination that 160 boys would wait in line for a bicycle ride. They were well behaved and excited with the sport. Mr. Skinas informed me that every Saturday he gave each boarder an allowance of twenty-five drachmas, equivalent to a half-dollar. "My children, instead of buying ice cream, they rented a bicycle." He chuckled and said, "So I bought them a used bike. Now, they can have a ride here on the premises and buy ice cream with their pocket money." It was an amazing sight to behold the excitement of these boys sharing one bicycle. *What would our American children say if they saw such joy over such a simple plaything?* I wondered.

When I returned to my post, which was now at St. Sophia Cathedral in Los Angeles, the image of what I had witnessed at the orphanage continued to be vivid in my mind. On Sunday morning, the picture continued to haunt me. I looked at my well-fed and well-dressed congregation—men, women, and children. I was about to deliver the Sunday sermon, and I could see from the jovial faces that the members were looking forward to my message.

Christmas was less than a month away. Knowing most of the congregation was involved in the frenzy of shopping, partying, and gift-buying, I thought of delivering a couple of brief messages about the mission of the church, focusing on God's love and charity. I could remind my audience of the needs of others and our Christian responsibility. When I mentioned my visit to the orphanage and their dire need for a refrigerator, I noticed some discomfort. I remember saying, "The Kingdom of God is not just in heaven after we die. It starts here, as we apply Christ's command: *Thy kingdom come.* As we repeat these three words, we become members of his kingdom now, and that means, we have to share God's gifts—our wealth and talents—with the less fortunate while we are still in this life."

That afternoon I received a telephone call from Despina, an eighty-five-year-old widow. She offered to buy the refrigerator. Roy Dolley, a convert who happened to be in the cathedral, also heard my sermon. A couple of days later, he visited my office and offered to build an additional dormitory so the boys would have more comfortable sleeping arrangements. Unfortunately, a week later, before Roy Dolley finalized his plans, he had a head-on collision on the Hollywood Freeway and died instantly.

Relatives and friends sent flowers to the mortuary. Sixty-seven wreaths, the funeral director told me. During the eulogy, I praised Roy Dolley's philanthropic intentions and told the listeners what he had planned to do for the orphanage. I thanked those who had sent flowers to honor him. Thinking about what happens to the flowers after the funeral, I said, "How wonderful it would be if, instead of spending so much money on flowers, we appropriated part of it for charity. Holy Days are around the corner, and the less fortunate would welcome help."

That was not what the trustees of the cathedral wanted to hear. After the funeral service, one of the trustees came to see me at my office. Arrogantly, he pillared himself in front of my desk and pointing his finger at me, he said, "If you ever speak like that again at any of the funerals of my friends, you will no longer belong to this cathedral."

Blood rushed to my face, and I tried hard to control my wrath. "What was so offensive to you?" I asked.

"You spoke about what interests you, charity and orphans."

"Is that so bad for a Christian congregation to hear?"

"Yes, we have national charities; they take care of these people."

I looked him straight in the eyes and said, "I am a priest, and an important part of my ministry is to direct our people to love each other and to practice charity."

"This congregation consists of good and generous people who have their own favorite charities. They don't need to be told what to do with their money. So, for your sake, I advise you to follow the wishes of the Board of Trustees."

I knew that this man had no power over me, but I had a hunch he could influence my local bishop and have me transferred. So be it! As inconvenient as a transfer would be, I still had myself and my perceptions to bring to another community. Thus far, I understood the church to be a clinic to provide help and healing. Through their brokenness, people came to church to experience God's grace, acceptance, and unconditional love. Networking with each other made possible that special feeling of brotherliness and sisterliness, expanding to reach out and touch other brothers and sisters.

The spirit of the cathedral congregation was not always that of networking. Charity was not in their charter. To a great degree, the Hollywood influence was evident in their appearance and lifestyle. Life was taken lightly. Living in a capitalistic society, most people found it hard to discover their own spiritual dimension. Affluence brought high fashion and style into their lives, but what inner joy did they experience? Yet who was I to judge? I could only evaluate silently what I saw. Joy is an inside job, and when we expect to find it outside, we end up disappointed. Perhaps, the yearning of their souls to reach out was stifled by material accumulations.

Performing the Sunday services and sacraments well was what most people expected of me. It was a visible part of my ministry, but I expected more of myself that was not visible to anyone but God. Besides parish duties, I began to follow a more gratifying path, that of domestic and foreign missionary work. If I were to keep my integrity intact, I had to obey my inner voice. I felt it was in sync with Christ's expectation of me, Matthew 28:19: "Go...and [teach] them to obey everything I have commanded you. And remember, I am with you always."

My involvement in educational activities, in missions and in the healing ministry of the church left very little time for my family. I became everybody's benevolent Father, but not a good father or husband at home. My wife and children complained about my long hours at work, and I began to envy my Catholic colleagues for being celibate. They had as much time as they needed to do things that they wanted, without the responsibility of a wife and children. Yet, I had no regrets that I had married. It was fun to come home to a wife and children. They, too, had a great deal to contribute.

Lessons I Have Learned

- A major step toward maturity and a healthier life is the realization and acceptance of who we really are. We are God's children. With this realization we can move on to attain what we need, and what our inner self requires. It is important to be discreet about our desires. We cannot always have what we want, and if a particular want should happen to be fulfilled, it may not be as important as we thought.

- The next step is to discover or rediscover what our purpose in life is. Do we want to be simply takers or do we want to be givers? Life is about giving, and it is in giving that we receive. Any contribution we can make, even as simple as giving a glass of cold water to a thirsty person, brings a smile of joy.

- As we get older, we become more aware of what we love and what we loathe. We can make new choices to pursue what is beneficial in our life, and we can avoid what appears to be catastrophic. Any choice that we make brings with it responsibility and work.

- We all want to be loved and to love, but as a rule we do not know how to love in a proper way. How should we love so that joyful living will really come from it? I believe that what we need is wisdom: a synthesis of thoughts, emotions, and logic. It is disappointing that our educational systems, and even our church, provide education but very little wisdom.

- In our middle-aged years we raise major questions: *What have we accomplished thus far? What have we failed to accomplish? In what direction should we travel from this point on?* Necessary changes usually require accurate information, careful planning, and diligent effort.

- Most humans have a tendency to judge themselves and others. We tear ourselves apart. We separate ourselves into the part that passes judgment and the part that gets judged. Our challenge is to find a way to bring those pieces back together again. The only way I know is to accept God's unconditional grace and love.

Additional Thoughts

As our journey of life continues, we mature along the way and rediscover who we really are. Then we take calculated steps to pursue what we want. What is it that we want? What kind of a decision or action do we need to perform to attain what we want? What results do we expect—power, prestige, pleasure, happiness? We ought to consider the difference between *wanting* and *needing* something. If we find ourselves passionately attached to a goal, it may be most effective to examine first our thoughts, and how we would feel if we did not achieve that goal. Already most of us have some wisdom and knowledge within us. We need to stop listening to external voices and listen to our own inner guide, our soul. It is available as we connect with our spiritual dimension, and trust in God who gives each of us breath and the heartbeat of life.

A Big Heart

We can enter the world with greater strength when our inten-
tion is noble and pertains to common good. We don't have to
prove anything, we don't have to defend anything. The results
are our responsibility.   —Richard Rohr

Between the years of 1965 and 1967 arrangements were
made for three children, aged seven and eight, to be sent from
Greece to St. Vincent's Hospital in Los Angeles. Johnny, Petrakis,
and Billy suffered from congenital heart failure and needed
open-heart surgery; otherwise their days were numbered. My part
was to coordinate this mission. The Ladies Philoptochos Society,
a philanthropic organization of the Orthodox Church, had
assumed the responsibility for all hospital and medical expenses.

At that time, open-heart surgery was not done in Greece, as
the doctors had not yet sufficient knowledge in the techniques.
Petrakis survived the operation and weeks later happily returned
to his homeland. The other two little boys unfortunately did not
make it. The tragic sight of Johnny's slow death and his incon-
solable mother standing next to him has never faded from my
mind. I remember how happy he was playing with my son Mike.
And one day he was no longer there. Even today, it continues to
haunt me, and I am still faced with the unanswerable question:
Why do innocent children have to die?

On the day of little Johnny's funeral, there was an article in
the *Los Angeles Times* stating that a team of cardiac surgeons had
just returned from Pakistan where they had donated their ser-

vices to the critically ill. They had performed forty-three open-heart surgeries with forty-one successes. These were missionary doctors from Loma Linda University Hospital (LLUH) in Loma Linda, California. *Maybe they can perform the surgery for Greek children,* I thought. That same afternoon I telephoned LLUH and asked to speak to the head doctor in charge of the heart team. Dr. Ellsworth Wareham came to the phone, and I mentioned how moved I felt when I read in the *LA Times* of the contribution his team had made to the people of Pakistan. Briefly I related my experience with the two boys who had died, and I asked if his team would consider going to Greece.

I could not believe my ears. He responded humbly and compassionately to my call. "Father"—everybody called me Father in those days "—you are a busy man. I shall come to your office, and we will discuss your request." That day I thought, *The spirit that nourishes every human soul visited with me, chanting the compassionate song of God's presence in human life.*

Soon afterward, Dr. Wareham came to my office, and we spent two hours discussing the possibility of his heart team going to Greece. A summary of his own words: "A team of seven of us will be able to go to Greece. We will donate our services, and all you have to do is provide for our traveling expenses."

I promised him there would be no problem in getting airplane tickets to Greece. *That will be the easiest thing to do,* I thought, and I immediately contacted Olympic Airways in New York and related Dr. Wareham's generous offer. "We need a contribution of seven round-trip tickets to Athens," I said. My request was denied with a brief answer: "It is with regret we inform you it is against IATA rules and regulations to give free air transportation to any individual or organization."

At that time, being a man of the cloth, I had to request permission from the head of the church to pursue this project. I wrote a letter to the archbishop explaining the situation, and his reply was, "Let me remind you that you are a priest, a spiritual leader whose commitment is to save the souls of his congregation. Involvement with doctors and medical problems is not a church issue. Besides, we have no church representative in Greece to supervise such a project."

The cardiac surgeons did not need ecclesiastical supervision. But by this time I had learned that when you try to do something worthwhile, obstacles are always put in your way. Even this humanitarian effort, promising health and hope to hundreds of heart victims, had to overcome two major obstacles: Olympic Airways' refusal to give free transportation, and the church hierarchy's refusal to allow me to pursue this mission.

How could I tell Dr. Wareham that two of my own resources had turned me down? I tried to find meaning in their refusal to help, but I could not. *There has to be another way,* I thought. My frustration ignited a fire within, an insistent call. I had to find a way to improvise funds for transportation. The wealth of the church, whose generosity made headlines in the news and who had erected monuments to themselves, could not extend a hand to help a monumental project! They referred me to charities. Wonderful!

Why not contact a Greek hospital in Athens? I thought. When I called to explain the offer by the American doctors, President Dr. Doxiades of Evangelismos Hospital felt offended. "We don't accept charity. We are not an underdeveloped country, and we don't need foreign medical help. We have here our own competent professionals." His laconic answer shut the door. I put my trust in the old axiom, "When one door closes, God opens ten new doors." Each negative answer became a strong step of patience cemented by persistence and prayer.

Prayer is my daily practice; patience is my passion and continues to be my best quality. I contacted Rebeccah Weiler, a compassionate candy striper, who happened to be at the hospital on the day little Johnny died. She was there to comfort the grieving mother. I mentioned the *LA Times* article about the missionary doctors. I told her I had spoken to the head doctor and that a team was ready and willing to go to Greece. "However, there is a problem," I said. "I have to provide transportation for them, and so far I have not been able to find even one person interested in helping." Without hesitation, Rebeccah said, "Don't worry. I'll pay for one ticket. I'm sure other donors will come forward." The following day, I received in the mail a travel ticket from El Al Airline. I was excited. Now I knew what the next step should be.

I must fly to New York, visit the headquarters of Olympic Airways, and explain the situation in person.

Correspondence, overnight letters, phone calls, and telegrams only delay results. Could emergency patients wait? "The face is like a sword," says a Greek proverb, meaning it cuts where it should and brings results. For me, the proverb meant that I needed to see these authorities in person and say to them: "We have many requests from heart patients in Greece who need heart surgery. They cannot afford to travel to America for help. Surgical intervention is now available, and we have a unique opportunity to help. The Loma Linda University Heart Team is volunteering its services at no charge. All we need is transportation and moral support."

To overcome barriers and get results, I needed divine intervention. On my way to visit the Olympic Airways office on Fifth Avenue, I prayed as I passed St. Patrick's Cathedral.

Mr. Love, the manager of the airline, stood behind his elegant desk and gave me an artificial smile as he offered me a chair. "What can I do for you, Father?" Not knowing my name, he could tell by my black suit and the white collar that I was a priest.

"Something very simple, Mr. Love," I said and explained the purpose of my visit.

"Of course, I remember. You contacted us about donating tickets."

"Transportation for doctors to save lives," I said.

"Sorry, but my hands are tied. There are rules I have to follow."

"Rules to deprive hope and health to people who suffer from heart failure?"

"Well, I could possibly give a personal donation, but tickets—that I cannot do."

"I know for a fact that you provide free transportation for celebrities."

"I have nothing to do with that," he said in an unyielding tone.

I pulled out the ticket from El Al, and I said, "I have a ticket donated by a Jewish lady, Rebecca Weiler. If you are unable to donate six more tickets, I will go from this office directly to El Al and ask for a donation. Once we arrive in Athens, I'll write an article in the Greek newspaper and tell them our story."

"I don't think Mr. Onassis would like that," Mr. Love said, coughing nervously. Aristotle Onassis owned Olympic Airways. He was also one of the richest people in the world.

"I don't think he'll like it either," I said.

My eyes no doubt flamed with frustration. My face was red. My hand holding the El Al ticket trembled as I waved it in Mr. Love's face. A priest ignited by anger was not in vogue. On the other hand, Mr. Love belonged to a society that followed the trends of the day: indifference and apathy. He probably enjoyed sitting back, watching sports, attending cocktail parties, flattering, smiling, and exchanging irrelevant stories.

I had not visited Mr. Love's office to change the rules of his company or his lifestyle. I had a purpose and a passion that required fulfillment. I did not feel enslaved to my passion, but the offer of the Loma Linda University Heart Team fired my soul. I felt alive when caring and serving the needs of others. Already I visualized the indigenous of Greece having a healthier life, and I was convinced that the process ought to be pursued in spite of obstacles. I sat opposite Mr. Love; he was one of those men who could not grab life's opportunity with his bare hands and relish it willingly. Instead, he handled it with tongs. He shuffled papers on his desk. I said not another word, but I kept looking straight in his eyes. Silently I repeated, *Lord Jesus Christ, have mercy on him and lead a good thought into his mind that he may actualize the true meaning of his last name, Love.* I had decided not to leave his office until I got favorable action.

Noticing my persistence, Mr. Love said dispassionately, "Let me have the names of these doctors, and I'll see if I can do anything. I'll call your office tomorrow." Somehow, I had a hunch that he might eventually give me the tickets.

I thanked him, and with my enthusiasm rekindled, I headed toward the New York City archdiocesan office on 79th Street and Fifth Avenue. Because I operated under the auspices of the church, it was imperative to inform the archbishop that we now had transportation, and the heart team would soon be on its way. I would be going with them as a liaison, but I had decided to buy my own ticket. I did not want to give the impression that my involvement had the ulterior motive of a free trip.

It so happened that I met the archbishop in the lobby. He was waiting for the elevator. I bowed and greeted him. He responded gently and said, "What brings you to New York?"

"Your Eminence, may I speak to you for a few minutes in private?"

"Today I have a very busy schedule. Tell me briefly what you want," he said as he held the elevator door open.

"It's about the heart mission—the outreach ministry to Greece."

"I thought I had answered your request in writing. Did I not?"

"Yes, you did, your Eminence. Now we are almost ready to go."

"Well, I have already spoken with the Greek government. They are not ready to receive the American doctors; perhaps they will be more receptive sometime in the future," he said with evident annoyance. He entered the elevator, pressed the button, and the door shut in my face.

I could not follow him to his office and try to convince him to see this effort as a call from God. Facing reality, which radically belied that everything I believed was possible, I now had four choices: I could deny what had happened in the past—perhaps by telling myself I'd had a momentary lapse of sanity—and keep a grim hold on my known world. I could accept what had happened, and compartmentalize it so that it would not affect my other beliefs, thereby believing and not believing at the same time. I could let bittersweet memories permeate my entire consciousness so that every belief I held dear would have to shift a bit.

Or, at the risk of being suspended or expelled from the ranks of the priesthood, I could disregard the archbishop's negative answer and continue to follow the orders of my own soul.

In spite of such strong resistance, on so many sides, I pressed on with the outreach ministry. I made all possible efforts to safeguard my own sanity and to preserve peace in my own family. At that time, I was blessed by the birth of a third child, and as I watched him grow, my love for children increased. The power to love is God's greatest gift to humans. In its true meaning, love can never be taken away from the ones that we genuinely love.

Finally, on November 1, 1967, Olympic Airways flew us to Greece, and we didn't have to dance in the aisles. Soon after our arrival at the Evangelismos Hospital in Athens, the doctors examined the heart patients. The candidates for open-heart surgery were many, and a day later the operations began. Within six weeks, thirty-two patients had surgery and twenty-nine of the operations were successful. The doctors compiled a list of eight-hundred patients who needed heart surgery within two years, otherwise they would die.

The heart team returned to Loma Linda University Hospital, and I was transferred from the cathedral to Westfield, New Jersey, to start a new parish. Six months passed swiftly as I performed my church work, but my thoughts kept gravitating to those people in Greece suffering from heart problems. They were awaiting a miracle, and I felt responsible that the mission remained unfinished. Now that I was three thousand miles away from those wonderful doctors in California, what could I do? I could pray, but would my prayers be enough? As powerful as prayer can be, God wants us to be active participants in whatever requests we make of him. Along with my prayers, I had to move on with that inner call, the flame that would brighten many lives with health and hope. I called Doctor Wareham one evening and said, "When I think of those eight hundred people who need surgery, I have sleepless nights."

"I understand totally," Dr. Wareham said.

"Do you think your team could go back to Greece again?" I asked hesitantly.

"It's possible, but you might have to come to Loma Linda and speak to Doctor Hinshaw, dean of the university. He is the one that would have to approve another mission."

"No problem," I said, and the following week I took an airplane to Los Angeles and from there, a smaller plane flying to Red Banks. The hospital was not far from the airport, and Dr. Wareham picked me up. That night I had a chance to speak at a dinner honoring the seven doctors for their major contribution to the Greek people. Besides expressing gratitude on behalf of the patients, I emphasized the fact that Greek hospitals and doctors were not yet equipped to do open-heart surgery, and they still needed American help.

After dinner that night, Dr. Wareham and his team met with Dr. Hinshaw and discussed the seriousness of their mission and the plight of the eight hundred Greek patients who were awaiting surgery. Their decision was announced to me next morning by Dr. Wareham: "A team of twelve doctors will go back to Greece to continue our work, train local doctors, and establish a permanent heart team there." I was overwhelmed by their second offer, and tears of joy filled my eyes. Dr. Wareham put his arms around me and said, "Now, Father, we need *twelve* tickets." He smiled. "I know you will be able to get them."

Back in New York at the Olympic office, Mr. Love caused waves. "We did it once—against our regulations—and we were criticized by other airlines. This time we cannot do it." Disheartened, I left his office. "Lord God," I whispered, "patients and doctors are now in your hands." Suddenly I saw Mr. Aristotle Onassis walking down the hall of his building. I had not met this man before, but I had seen his picture in the newspapers when he had married Jacqueline Kennedy. He was a short man of dark complexion, and he was the giant multimillionaire who owned Olympic Airlines. I introduced myself. "Mr. Onassis," I said, "Thank you very much for providing transportation for the doctors."

"You're welcome. You're welcome," he said and sped away before I had a chance to say, "We need additional help." One of his consultants informed me: "Mr. Onassis is not to be bothered at this time." The high-powered businessman had come to New York on that particular day to discuss the purchase of more oil wells for his shipping fleet. I had to understand that, despite his generosity, the great tycoon of wealth and fame also had his own priorities.

Late in the afternoon, I composed a letter to Mrs. Jacqueline Onassis and sent it by overnight mail to her Fifth Avenue apartment. I explained in detail the success of the first mission to Greece, and I requested her intervention for twelve more tickets to enable the doctors to go a second time to attend to the patients. The next morning around ten o'clock, my telephone rang. It was Mr. Love.

"Good morning, Father. How are you?"

"Indisposed. I had a sleepless night, Mr. Love," I said, with evident frustration.

"You're too emotional, Father. But the news I have to tell you will perk you up."

"I'm listening."

"This morning, Mrs. Onassis forwarded your letter to me. Your twelve tickets will be ready by this afternoon, and there will be a ticket for you as well, if you decide to go with the doctors."

"Thank you, Mr. Love. I will be there this afternoon to give you the names of the doctors." I went next door immediately and knelt at the altar. "Thank You, Lord, for another miracle."

At this juncture, it is important to acknowledge the generosity and sensitivity of the female heart. Throughout history women have been active participants in church life. Their inspiration and dedication date back to the time of Christ. During his crucifixion, they showed unconditional compassion, courage, and strength. They were there. Not only did they stand by the cross offering comfort until the end, but right after the Sabbath, at dawn, unafraid of the threatening consequences, they went to the tomb to pay their last respects to their teacher.

Most church leaders today will admit how substantial the contribution of women is to their ministry. When women hear of an existing need, they are eager and ready to help. Knowing of their consistent commitment to charity, I sent a letter to each state chapter of the Philoptochos Ladies Society informing them of the "heart mission" to Greece.

Once again women proved to be the proponents of the Christian spirit. Within a month, they sent $68,000 to their main office in New York for the heart mission. In those days, this was a hefty amount of money. It helped to buy a heart-lung machine, a stryker saw used to cut open the sternum, and other surgical tools. Above all, it helped to continue the service of the American heart-menders for five years, until they trained local Greek doctors to take over this much-needed project.

From that day on and for the following three years, a rotating team of heart specialists from Loma Linda University Hospital went to Greece. Every four weeks, four new doctors arrived to relieve them, and the system ran like clockwork. In the interim, local surgeons were trained to do the work, and George Tolis, a Greek doctor who had been trained in Cleveland, Ohio, was assigned head of the heart team. The American heart team did not have to remain in Athens as the Greek team became competent. The mission of the Loma Linda team was complete.

___◌___◌___

In the interim, I had asked Dr. Wareham to prepare a prospectus describing what it would take to build a hundred-bed clinic in Athens.

A tiny acorn, planted at the right time in the right soil, produces a huge oak tree. In his will, Aristotle Onassis left instructions that a heart clinic be established in Greece. Years after his death, his instructions were carefully carried out. In the year 2000, Dr. Wareham returned to Greece with his wife, Barbara. When they came back, he called me from New York and asked me to meet him for lunch at the Essex House. I had not seen the man in more than twenty years, but he looked as lively and as healthy as ever, and was very excited to tell me the latest news

"Dr. Kalellis, there is no hospital in the world, as far as I know, that does such an efficient service as the Onassis Cardiovascular Center in Athens. I spent two days there, exploring it and learning about its functions. They perform approximately two thousand operations a year, something that no other hospital can do even in the United States. It is a miracle of human endeavor."

"Thanks to you and to your team," I said.

"We can thank God for enabling us to do his work," he said.

I could not argue with that. I looked at him with admiration and reminded him of the initial obstacles we encountered when we first went to Athens—professional jealousy on the part of their Greek colleagues, not enough surgical tools, red tape, and bureaucracy—but Dr. Wareham didn't seem to remember what he called "small stuff."

"What obstacles?" he said with a smile.

I reminded him of the day there was no blood available—and they always needed to supplement blood for each operation.

"We cannot have any surgery tomorrow," Dr. Stathatos, head of the Thoracic Surgery Department, had said.

Dr. Wareham had then looked at the faces of his team and said, "Oh, well! All of us look very healthy here; *we* will donate blood."

Silence prevailed for a few seconds, succeeded by smiles. Sure enough, the surgery continued the next day.

At the end of the day, after witnessing two major operations, I stepped out of the hospital for a few minutes to catch a breath of fresh air. A long line of young soldiers waited at the main entrance. "What's the meaning of this? I asked, and they answered, "We are here to give blood."

"You are smiling, and you are silent," Dr. Wareham said now.

"Not silent. Grateful," I replied. I kept thinking of a doctor, a priest, a candy striper, and—may God rest her soul—Jacqueline Kennedy Onassis—and how each of them responded to tragedy.

According to the wishes of the benefactor, the hospital delivers contemporary cardiovascular care to Greece and also to the international community. The services include preventive medicine, diagnosis, and treatment of all forms of acquired and congenital heart diseases. In 2002, Dr. Ellsworth Wareham reported on the state of the facility: "The hospital consists of highly trained medical and nursing staff that offer quality care according to individual needs and lifestyles. An efficient administrative infrastructure coordinates all activities." The picture of the benefactor, Aristotle Onassis, hangs in the main entrance to the hospital. Although Aristotle Onassis is no longer alive, his tremendous contribution, the untiring and dedicated service of Dr. Wareham, and ongoing power of the Holy Spirit will continue to make it possible to offer health care for the years to come.

Lessons I Have Learned

- When we believe in something, we must pursue it with faith and conviction, without necessarily calculating what the payoff is for us.

- Realizing that time passes by faster than we like to believe, we learn to think before we act, and we weigh matters carefully. An ancient axiom advises: *Make haste slowly.* We must be patient. Acting or reacting compulsively, before thinking through the details of a situation, can produce results that make life difficult and perhaps destructive.

- Like the flame of a candle that brings light into a dark room, our good thoughts can illuminate our dark and hidden facets. As scripture suggests, we can let our good works shine that others can see and glorify our Father in heaven. Using sensitivity, allowing our good thoughts to guide us, and moving forward cautiously, we can choose to do what needs to be done—God's work.

- We are capable people, and we should not hesitate to pursue our desired goal with confidence, courage, and love in our hearts. When opposing forces present us with obstacles, we can use these obstacles as stepping stones to climb to a higher level of existence so that we can visualize the future with optimism.

- As we interact with other people, we require understanding of their reality; it is not our job to pronounce judgment, and we must be prepared to use a super dose of patience. At times, even our altruistic intentions—trying to help a philanthropic cause and caring for individuals in need—may be met with disappointment.

- Episodes in the course of our life—successes, failures, joys, sorrows, tragedies—need to be recounted so that others may ponder on them and perhaps extract from them something useful in their own lives.

Additional Thoughts

When we see or hear about pain, calamity, hunger, slavery, or suffering, we sympathize, we make contributions, and we feel good knowing the hungry will be fed and the sick will receive medical attention.

The poor of the world do not have the luxury of assuming that unneeded things will offer them fulfillment. They do not have access to them; they have to find life at a cheap, immediate, and simple level—often just food, clothes, and shelter. This situation puts them at an unimaginable disadvantage, but in the Sermon on the Mount, Christ states, "Blessed are the poor." They may have very little of earthly goods, but they are rich in God's presence in their lives.

10

Facing Reality

*Going all the way back to childhood we recall the earliest expe-
riences which involved endings, vivid memories of happiness
or sadness. Everyone finds endings confusing, difficult and
fearful. However, as we mature and learn to deal with these
endings, we make viable transitions.*   —William Bridges

Another seven years and another birthday passed. I was
seven-times-seven years old—forty-nine. During this most recent
seven-year period, two major events shook the foundation of my
life. A double divorce took place almost simultaneously: the dissolution of my marriage of twenty-one years was followed by my
departure from the church that I had served for twenty-two years.

Divorce ends a marriage but not a relationship. Memories live
on to haunt the survivors, who ever seek some resolution that may
never come. Over several weeks, many confusing thoughts and
painful emotions tumbled through my mind and heart. I did not
know how to approach my children and tell them I would no
longer be living at home with them and their mother. No child of
any age or gender can really understand what a divorce implies.
Children want love, security, and warmth. They want both parents
to remain together and offer a climate of comfort and support
until they embark on their own journeys through life. Would they
believe my promise that I would not disappear from their lives and
that I would be around to attend to their needs? I did not think so.

When my then wife heard of my decision, she was shocked.
She pleaded with me and cried: "I don't want a divorce!" Her

reaction evoked deep guilt within me. I had no convincing answers that could justify my decision, yet repairing the relationship no longer seemed possible. In time, she and I had to face the reality that somehow we both contributed to the emotional breakup. Since each one of us would be heading in a different direction, we could individually rethink at what point we had failed, and perhaps learn something about ourselves. At crossroads, usually new decisions need to be made, requiring a challenge, a risk, and the ability to face the consequences.

How I was going to face the world and respond to public opinions were not my priorities. A decision had been made, and it was time for responsible action. Loss of security was a major concern; all the family income came from my church ministry, and I expected I would soon be without employment. I needed to provide financial and emotional support for my family. When I consciously realized the despair that my decision had caused, I also realized how inefficient and irrelevant my answers were. Had either one of us died, it would have been easier. At the funeral, the surviving spouse would wear dark glasses, shed real tears, and take the children aside to comfort them. In view of the current situation, I could only stand by my children, be present and supportive in their life, and pray for healing.

My experience indicates that, most of the time, we make certain decisions on a deeper level. When the decision implies serious consequences, we go through a state of ambivalence and confusion. Because indecision causes inaction and mental paralysis, eventually we make a decision that seems to promise a future. I was aware that the emotional divorce had taken place long before my final decision. But the implementation was the most difficult part and needed serious consideration. It seemed that I had entered a new country without passport, directions, or maps, and I entered it absolutely alone. It was a strange land, and I had to make my own roads as I walked and choose my own landmarks. Insanity or hopelessness was a natural product of that land.

One day, I isolated myself in a small room for a long time. I lit a candle, and performed my own funeral. It was a genuine metaphor—a major part of my life had died, possibly taking with it my yesterdays. I was consciously aware of what was taking place within me. As ridiculous as it may sound, I chanted a brief ritual and gave myself a eulogy. Mainly I spoke the truth about myself as I perceived it: the wrongs I had done, the sins and unwitting errors I had committed. I asked God for forgiveness. The eulogy was one of the few acts I had to go through that would change my life completely.

In reconstructing my life, facing the truth about myself was necessary but not sufficient. Truth alone does not determine whether or not we should look for cause, choice, or justification. Two stories of the same event, related by two different people, may be radically different yet equally true. A person's own point of view is what he or she perceives to be truth. Truth does not necessarily provide the criterion for a justified answer.

My own perception of what precipitated the divorce was determined by personal disenchantment about the life I was living, and by possible plans for a different lifestyle that I had visualized. *If you do not want to consider yourself a failure,* I told myself, *you need to do some self-repair work, face the truth about who you are, chisel off the rough edges, and become a better person.* Once again, it was time to look at myself carefully to find what I had missed, to understand the reality of married life and the mystery of being human.

In any case, most professionals in the field of marital therapy would agree that it takes two people to make or break a relationship. We need to be aware of who we are, accept who we are, change what we need to change, adapt to new situations, and apply new methods to the experiences that lie ahead. This awareness will help us to create possible options, freedom of choice, and concerted responsibility to pursue our goals—*a newness of life.*

Think of a caterpillar. Its life begins as a tiny worm, which moves slowly on plants or trees, and eats tender leaves in order to grow. As a full-size caterpillar, it encloses itself in a cocoon and dies confined in darkness. In time, a colorful butterfly emerges from the cocoon and flies happily in the air, dancing from flower to flower. It is hard to imagine this miraculous transformation, how a worm becomes a butterfly. Like the caterpillar, human life starts slowly, and goes through variations and multiple experiences until full physical growth. The process of growth into adulthood tends to be troublesome. Critical circumstances change the way we think and feel. Our vision becomes blurred, and we can hardly see where we are going. After strenuous travel, we finally see light and find a new direction. Our physical appearance may remain intact, yet a transformation of our unseen part takes place: our inner self is transformed. Our thoughts, feelings, and actions are different. Like the butterfly, we jump from flower to flower, seeking the most colorful and fragrant one, *a newness of life* that promises purpose and meaning.

The painful transition and self-transformation that I was going through affected each member of my family, including myself. I knew the road ahead would be steep and thorny. I prayed for direction and for God's mercy, not to condone or approve my decision, but to give each member of my family the strength to endure the transition.

Abandoning the familiar for the unknown involved risks. I felt an acute anxiety as I witnessed the gradual dissolution of my current mode of existence, which fueled my fear of the final dissolution and insecurity. During the night, a disturbing nightmare would waken me out of my sleep. Early morning dreams terrorized me; my brain echoed the word *rectify*. Rectify what? The ruins of my marriage or the uncertainty of my future? Did I have the desire, stamina, or skills to repair anything? Can a crack in a window be repaired? At best, the glass can be replaced. I simply reacted to what was happening in my psyche. Confusion, guilt, and worries about the future! Slowly, I learned to live with the insecurity of the unknown and tolerate the events of life as they occurred.

Epictetus, a Greek philosopher, said that humans are influenced and disturbed not by the events of their lives but by the way they view or interpret the events. In reexamining that thought, I began to focus on how I viewed the immediate world around me, my own family, and how I defined my divorce and my likely departure from the church. Had I been a runner and lost a leg, I would have accepted that I could no longer run and could learn how to swim. I would have to accept my loss and learn to live with it. It was reality I had to face, to provide for my children and their mother a life of reasonable financial support and stability. The breakup was a long period of anxiety, emotionally painful and scarring for the entire family.

My mind still wrestled with the ambivalence, yet I needed to take charge of my life. Selfishly, I had to deal with my fragmented self and regain composure. How did I do it? I sensed an inner impasse and felt deep grief, fear, despair, and loneliness. But I had no desire to be lonely or alone the rest of my life. I prayed to God for help. I cried. I knew that I was crying about my losses: people I loved, the love of my family, and the security of a high position in society, my church.

Of course, somewhere in the midst of despair, there is always a ray of relief. A young woman named Pat had already become an active part of my ministry, helping in areas that harmonized and promoted philanthropic endeavors. In her presence, questions about my commitments to my family and church, and what tragedy I was causing, demanded answers. I wanted Pat to be my lifetime companion. I did not want her to withdraw from my life. She appeared to be an anchor of hope and a source of true comfort. Of course, I could not use her or any other excuse to diffuse my misery or to escape my responsibilities. I had to accept that this emotional mess was my fault, and it was time for me to do something about it.

During this time, I was still taking courses in psychology, and I began to write a self-help book, now published under the title *Twenty Secrets for Healing Thoughts, Feelings, and Relationships*. The journey through writing this book proved to be a therapeutic experience that provided healing and eventually led to new horizons.

God does not have human hands to embrace us and to show us that he loves us, even when we fail him. But he sends angels, loving and caring people, to bring his love into our life. When colleagues—priests who knew me for many years—heard about my situation, they offered help, but they were in a quandary. One of my classmates in the school of psychology was Rabbi Joseph Goldman, who has become a lifetime friend. He and his wife, Sally, offered their home if I needed a place to reside. I'll never forget their kindness.

Another caring angel stood out in his generosity. He was my neighbor, the late Monsignor Charles Murphy, and he went out of his way to provide immeasurable comfort. Obviously he knew the heartaches that are ahead of a man who leaves the church.

When he heard my story, he offered me substantial help. He put his gracious arm around me and whispered, "You are one of our brothers, and we'll do anything in our power to help you."

This unexpected offer left me in tears. Rarely had I seen such generosity. I was a member of the Greek Orthodox Church, and here was a Roman Catholic priest who called me his brother. Monsignor Murphy was in touch with human pain. He did not indulge in theological abstractions or judgmental thinking. On the contrary, he tried to be available to me when I needed someone to talk to, although I was already in professional psychotherapy. His presence emanated a warmth and love that only Christ made available to sinners. When he sensed guilt in my voice, he comforted me with genuine compassion. Although a celibate, he knew enough about children's reactions to their parents divorcing. He said, "Inevitably your children are going to be angry with you. They may find it hard to forgive you; they may even refuse to see you or talk to you. It is a normal reaction. Be patient and don't let that be an obstacle. All I suggest is talk to them gently, be emotionally available, and let them know where you live and how they can get in touch with you. Give them a phone number that they may call whenever they need you. Take them to places where they would like to go; go with them to a movie or to a good restaurant. Avoid blaming or deriding their mother or defending your decision."

When Monsignor Murphy felt reassured of my appreciation of his hospitality, with a gracious smile he said, "Peter, you are a middle-aged man, and most likely, you will marry again someday, perhaps marry even a younger woman. It often happens. But your ex-wife, a mother with three kids, will probably have a hard time finding a mate. I'm sure she would prefer to be with your children. They, in turn, will be more supportive of their mother. Should you start a new family, don't expect your children to be happy about it. In the years to come, they may be able to accommodate, even accept, your new life. Leave that part in the hands of God. He always provides solutions."

As the years flew by, faster than I could ever imagine, my children accepted my new direction in life. I am grateful to God and to them, for we have developed a better relationship than we ever had before. Basil, my younger son, was my third child to get married. He met Yen Fen, the love of his life, in Taiwan. Soon after the wedding ceremony, along with our family wishes, I said, "Basil, it is my hope and prayer that what has happened in my life, the breakup of our family, will never happen to you."

Basil put his arms around me and, with glowing eyes, replied: "Dad, if what happened to you had not happened, I would never have traveled to such a far-away country to marry this wonderful woman whom I love dearly. I know she loves me, too. It is all in God's plan."

Truly, all of us live under the grace of God. We know we have a past, but we prefer to leave it behind us. It serves no purpose in our daily life, except to remind us of our human vulnerability. We learn from it, but we should not punish ourselves by continually regretting it. We can accept the past as past, without denying it or discarding it. At times we may reminisce about it but we must try not to live in it.

Today, my family and I firmly and lovingly stand by each other, and sometimes we travel overseas together. We share important aspects of life, major holidays and special dates. Either we meet in my home or theirs to celebrate each occasion as one family. As we break bread together, we talk and laugh and cherish each opportunity as God's bliss. How can I ever thank God, the Giver of All, for both the seen and unseen benefits that He has bestowed upon me over the years?

Lessons I Have Learned

- As we grope through the dark alleys of life, unable to discern direction in the midst of chaotic uncertainty, we realize that there is no way to repair a worn-out experience. When our resources diminish, we need someone, a friend or a therapist or a spiritual person who can mirror our current life. Such a mentor can help us recover the whole energy and potency that is inherent in our humanity.

- Expecting the children of divorcing or divorced parents to approve or understand their parents' divorce is a pipe dream. Regardless of how bad a marriage is or how angry the children may feel about their parents' behavior, deep down in their heart they hope and wish that their home would remain intact. Children need adult love and security.

- Children too make transitions as they grow. As their parents who brought them into the world, we must help them make these transitions by modeling good behavior and by doing more listening and less lecturing. Children's needs must be reasonably nurtured. Some parents who grew up in an emotionally deprived environment tend to overdo things for their children. Indulging them only maintains and enables their dependency.

- When a family breaks down, the result is a climate of confusion, pain, emptiness, and blurred vision. Things that used to be pleasurable and rewarding do not seem to matter anymore. Thoughts are negative, feelings are vague, actions are erratic. Members of a broken family have fears; they are lost in a great, dark nonworld. Some parents move on with their lives; others feel trapped and resist making a transition. Gradually, reality lights a candle, disperses darkness, and reveals the inevitable human vulnerability.

- When the light illuminates our human condition, the spirit within becomes the psychological obstetrician to whack us on the back and get us to admit the truth about who we really are and what we have done so far. This is perhaps one of the most difficult parts of our life, because admitting the truth hurts. Yet, arriving at this point and admitting the truth marks a new beginning.

- Daily I ponder and wrestle with Robert Browning's concept of truth. In his long poem *Paracelsus*, he writes:

Truth is within ourselves; it takes no rise
From outward things, whate'er you may believe.
There is an inmost center in us all,
Where truth abides in fullness; and around,
Wall upon wall, the gross flesh hems it in,
This perfect, clear perception—which is truth.

• On a deeper level and with an honest look within, we
do get a glimpse of what the truth is about us. It is
our human vulnerability that makes us ignore or
dilute the truth and accept our fantasies or illusions.
As a result, we live in a state of chronic dissatisfaction, still looking for the ideal, the promised land
that cannot be reached unless we face the truth
about who we really are in God's eyes.

Additional Thoughts

*Truth is a point; the subtlest and finest; harder than adamant;
never to be broken, worn away, or blunted. Its only bad quality is that it is sure to hurt those who touch it; and likely to
draw blood, perhaps the life blood, of those who press earnestly
upon it. It presupposes the Cross.*   —Walter S. Landor

11

Surrender

The little reed, bending to the force of the wind, soon stood upright again when the storm had passed.   —Aesop

I was out of work. I had taken a dive into deep waters, not totally considering the depth and my ability to rise and swim. My intended work and the Sunday liturgy remained unfinished. The church that I had loved all my life, which I had served diligently and creatively as priest, my symbolic mother, had no place for a man who had broken his marriage vows. The splendor of Byzantine iconography—the melodic music, and the fragrant incense that enveloped the altar every Sunday all were to fade away into oblivion. History does not record such emotionally painful events.

Divorced priests are persona non grata in a parish. The hierarchy could not possibly accept the idea of divorce for a priest, yet they want their priests to be married men, as if marriage is an absolutely faultless institution. In reality, how could the Orthodox hierarchs, who by church canons are celibate, know the ramifications of married life? Don't they realize that sometimes even clergy marriages can be dysfunctional? Does ordination to the priesthood make a man infallible? Shouldn't the church, as a loving and compassionate institution, be concerned and caring? Would an army officer ever ignore a wounded soldier?

On the parish level, insanity increased daily, devastating my life. Some parishioners, even those whose lives I had touched and helped to go through troublesome times, spread vicious gossip, lies, and slander. People whom I had served for years as their priest, whose children I had baptized and taught, and whose joy and sorrow I had shared distanced themselves. Some became mean in spirit and kept tattling about the scandal I had created. I did not defend myself against those taunting tongues that claimed absolute authority over my life. In such a hostile climate, defending myself served no purpose. It was sad to see that the Christian spirit had evaporated from some of the devout church-goers. They took it upon themselves to be my judges.

Periodically, I have the habit of opening the Bible and reading on a random page. One morning, my eyes fell on the familiar gospel story of a rich man and a poor beggar named Lazarus (Luke 16:19–31). Although I knew the story, I read it twice and kept asking myself, *What does it mean to me today?* In my own words, I will reiterate the story briefly:

> The rich man was clothed in purple and fine linen and feasted sumptuously every day. One day he died and was buried but he found himself tormented by flames. The selfish and insensitive use of his material prosperity caused his downfall, from temporary happiness to eternal misery. The beggar, who was satisfied each day to eat a few crumbs that fell from the rich man's table, also died, but he found himself in the arms of Abraham, a symbol of joy and lasting happiness.

Obviously, Jesus had a reason to tell this story to his audience, and it was not by coincidence that I happened to read it. At that moment, I closed my eyes and visualized myself sitting among the crowd in Jerusalem and listening to the gentle voice of Jesus. But what was he telling me? To which category did I belong? It seemed that his words were applicable to my personal life. Here I was, a parish priest clothed in colorful vestments every Sunday standing before the altar, endowed with a wealth of talents, and prominent among the clergy and laity, yet like the rich man, I ignored my priestly commitment. Self-absorbed, I succumbed to a grave error in judgment; in Greek, the word is *hamartia*—translated into English, the phrase is "tragic flaw." My life from the position of the highest calling—in the service of God—"reversed in blunder," *peripeteia,* so that I was now destined to be satisfied with the leftover crumbs, like the poor man Lazarus. In my own eyes, I had fallen from grace. I had broken the promise I had made at my ordination: *to preserve and carry the mission of Christ until the end of my life.* What did Christ think of me? Now I had no congregation, no pulpit, no family, no respect from people, I was in the company of the rich man in Hades. Tormented by guilty thoughts and regrets, I wished that someone would rescue me from the place of torment. It was of some relief to think of myself also as the poor man of the parable, eating crumbs that fell from the rich man's table; now I had a new life in the arms of Abraham, a foreshadow of happiness.

My fantasy was not a masochistic approach to my dilemma. It was rather a lifetime lesson about human consciousness that I had begun to grasp. It was a lesson that I could share. It helps to be aware and vigilant. Otherwise, how easy it would be, under like circumstances, to make a drastic change of direction, while ignoring consequences and public opinion. Good citizens—sane, normal people—do things against the rules. In moments of delusive ecstasy, they cast aside their vows and commitments. We hear of real-life situations where couples that have been married for years leave their spouses and children. They abandon all responsibilities, ruin careers and marriages to fulfill a dream or personal desire. I do not wish to throw stones or deride anyone or myself for making such a personal choice, but I am compelled to confront an almost unbearable truth: every folly or myopia of which any human being is guilty may be traced back to a serious aspect of our human nature. Humans are not perfect. They make mistakes. Success does not teach us a lasting lesson, as a mistake usually does.

I kept turning the gospel pages, and came to the Second Letter to Timothy. Paul, the apostle of reconciliation, offered abundant comfort and hope: "My child, be strong in the grace that is in Christ Jesus....Share in suffering like a good soldier of Christ Jesus. No one serving in the army gets entangled in everyday affairs; the soldier's aim is to please the enlisting officer....Think over what I say, for the Lord will give you understanding in all things" (2 Tim 2:1–7). In reading Paul's admonition to Timothy, I felt like a soldier, perhaps a wounded one, but I could still find a proper way to please Christ who had enlisted me in his army, and who would guide me. I believed that in his eyes, I was still a priest, and he would never abandon me.

If I acknowledged my own wrongdoing with a genuine regret, I could at least stay on the right track, making sincere efforts to rectify emotional damages I had caused. A verse from the Epistle of James encouraged me: "Draw near to God and he will draw near to you" (4:8). Christ had already set the example, as he approached people regardless of their sinful condition and entered their hearts with unconditional love. His nonjudgmental approach motivated them to live a new life, devoid of sin. I had to come closer to Christ that he might enter my heart and give me strength in my difficult situation.

If I said simply, "I'm sorry," to those whom my actions had offended, my guilt could generate self-judgment and negative thinking. Dwelling in my transgression could serve no other purpose than become a relentless source of punishment and self-induced suffering. I chose to let go of what had happened and visualized Christ extending a compassionate arm, embracing me and accepting me as the loving father had accepted his prodigal son. This process required a willingness to shed my persona—those inauthentic trappings I had carried in my mind that no longer served any purpose. If God forgives, who was I to deny his gift of love and forgiveness? My part was to let go, and forgive myself, if I were to regain peace, healing, and personal growth. Believing in God's grace I began to see that he had new plans for me.

Thank God for genuine friends. Many who knew of my work, especially those in the Department of Church Education that had accepted books I had authored and visual aids I had produced, remained supportive of me. Chuck Mogensen, a convert, provided me with a home, food, and a car to transport my belongings from the church office to his garage.

At the headquarters of the church, the archbishop stood adamantly behind his desk and said, "I am aware of your present situation. I want to know what plans you have for your future."

"I'm not sure, no definite plans yet," I said, thinking that he might be concerned.

"Ambivalence is unacceptable, Father," he said with a sad grimace. "You realize, I still call you *Father* in spite of the fact that you have abandoned the church." Clenching the jeweled pectoral cross on his chest, he spoke like a pontiff: "You are causing a great scandal in ecclesiastical circles."

Believing that nothing he could say would dampen God's heart toward me, I said, "I love our church, your Eminence."

"Show it in action. Repent and return to our church. Otherwise, write me a letter requesting your defrocking. In so doing, you will not be deprived of the grace of God."

I could have quoted St. Paul's words: "My grace is sufficient for you, for my power is made perfect in weakness" (2 Cor 12:9). I knew this kind of faith would set me free to be who I really was.

I had no wish to be a victim of this powerful man's attitude. I had problems to solve: I had no income at hand, and I had a family to support. I chose to align my thoughts, emotions, and actions with the highest part of myself—my soul. I had to get to know myself better—mentally, emotionally, physically, and spiritually—and fill my heart with enthusiasm, purpose, meaning, and a large dose of humility. Once we become aware of *who* we really are, we avoid justified or unjustified resentment and bitterness and live life to its fullest potential.

Lowering my eyes and my tone of voice, I said, "Your Eminence, I need to make a living."

"That is not a concern of the church. You have made a bad choice. What do you expect the church to do for you now?"

"I have done extensive work for the educational department of the archdiocese. I could work in that area, anonymously." *A reasonable income from the church might carry me through to the end of my studies in psychology,* I thought. I had another year of training, and then a new career as a psychologist lay ahead of me.

"The church is compassionate; that door shall remain open to you," he said.

"Thank you," I said, reaching for his hand. He pulled back and dialed a phone number. I took the hint; our dialogue was over.

I left his office, envisioning possibilities: *That door shall remain open to you.* Those were encouraging words. The following day I called the head of the Department of Religious Education and asked in what areas I could be of help. The priest in charge knew of my work; at one time he had assigned me a major project to be used for the Sunday school department. I was to produce a history of the church through a series of visual aids, accompanied by manuals. Teachers and students were pleased with the material. I was glad I had talent in that direction, and knew I could use it now to keep the wolf from the door.

"We should never count our chickens before they hatch." It was a bitter blow when the priest in charge confided in me that, the previous evening, the archbishop had given him the following order over the phone: *I don't want the Department of Religious Education to have any contact with Mr. Kalellis!*

Soon after, whatever publications or visual aids I had produced were removed from the Department of Religious Education.

"When it rains, it pours," says an old proverb, and I didn't have an umbrella. One winter night I returned home, and outside the front door were three big garbage bags containing most of my belongings—clothes, shoes, and books. The days that followed were dark, and yet within me I sensed energy, a life force that exists within survivors, an unleashing of vitality that needs to be translated into action. I did not feel sorry for myself, although during lonely nights, I prayed: *Lord, if there is a time to take me away, this would be a good time. As I go to sleep, take me away peacefully. I don't want to live any longer.* Apparently God had other plans for me.

Thinking about the injustices of life, wallowing in self-pity, or commiserating with others would have been a waste of energy. Feeling victimized by circumstances or feeling unfairly treated by others could only produce depression. To keep from feeling self-pity, I surrendered to three facts: life is not fair, it did not have to be, and my responsibility was to do something about it. It was my job to do everything in my power to improve my life and the world around me.

I had some knowledge and strength to deal with difficult decisions. Now I had to travel alone in search of a job. The search was not an easy task. I heard the same old responses over and over again: "You are overqualified or underqualified." "What could you possibly do for our company?" "Sorry!" The potential employers were right. What kind of job could they offer to a man approaching fifty who was trained only to be a priest? The fear of not finding employment began to creep into my thoughts, causing excruciating headaches and sleepless nights. Some people motivated by fear move on with life; they take risks. I had to be one of them. In spite of the fears for my future and the way I had designed my life, I tried not to degrade myself in my interaction with others. It was not easy to let go of my past assumptions about reality. The world appeared as a battlefield and required armor and struggle. Once I took off the clerical collar, I realized that my first task was to give up my prestigious priestly successes and expectations and adopt new ways. Whether I liked it or not, I was moving into a transition period with one hope, that tomorrow will be a better day.

The exile of Adam and Eve from the Garden of Eden became a metaphor of my life. Because of my personal choice, I had lost the sense of belonging and the feeling of security that the church provides. I had expelled myself from God's Garden of Eden, and there was no way to get back. As Moses had to cross the desert to reach the promised land, so, it was time for me to walk through the desert of my own reality. Imagine the conditions of crossing a desert—loneliness, rocks, thorns and thistles, scorpions and snakes, endless obstacles. Yet, we become convinced there is hope that promises a life ahead, a life that we can face and redesign responsibly.

God has a plan for each one of us that comes into this world. It depends upon us how we adjust and design our life as it unfolds in front of us. We might have to go through the desert experience, but our faith in a loving God who truly cares will bring us out of darkness. Under his light, we will realize his promising invitation, "Come closer to me," where we can find his love even if we are not lovable, where we can find forgiveness even when we feel unforgivable. Can we accept his compassionate invitation that is unconditional?

No matter how my own family felt, no matter how my cultural background, education, and church viewed my decision, I

106

had to make a new beginning. The Horacian axiom that whoever makes a beginning, has half of the job done, was of no comfort. It could be wishful thinking. Being in the neutral zone, how would I know which path before me represented a genuine beginning? I needed to start somewhere, somehow, but I needed, as a simple way out, a procedure to follow rather than a process to understand. All my life I have read different books for comfort and guidance, or to enhance my knowledge. Only lately had I discovered the inspirational writings of Henri J. M. Nouwen. While writing this chapter I picked up his book *Here and Now* and read the following lines:

> We must learn to live each day, each hour, each minute as a new beginning, as a unique opportunity to make everything new. The "oughts," the "shoulds," and the "what ifs" fill our minds. The past and the future keep harassing us. The past with regrets and guilt, the future with worries.

Suddenly, an old axiom surfaced in my mind: gradual wisdom of today, if I only had you yesterday. I wish I had known of Nouwen's wisdom during my trying times. His message disturbingly invades our bouts of ambivalence, uneasiness, frustration, insecurity, and confusion. All these feelings interwoven with guilt need to be reevaluated and put in perspective. How long could anyone swing between guilt and innocence, action and passivity? Where is our faith in a caring, loving, and forgiving God who is always present in our life? Did we place God on a throne too high above us, so our weak prayers cannot reach him? What is really happening to humankind, and what purpose does it serve to distance our life from God?

Struggling against my own self-doubts and insecurities, I had to emerge to become a normal and useful person in my own vision. Patience and perseverance were not enough. I had to understand and combat the furies within myself that subtly undermined my plans, casting doubt on my capabilities. Having spent the first twenty years of my life in Greece, I still carried fragments of the immigrant mentality. Scared and hesitant about any-

107

thing new and unfamiliar, I thought that the only way to survive was to use the early skills I had used when I returned to the United States twenty-nine years ago. Take each step the old, slow, safe way. While I had made many external changes, I still lived in the safety code that I was taught in my youth. *I'll take any job available, I don't mind washing dishes again, just as I did the first year in America. Honest work never scared me as long as I could have a decent meal, a place to live, and clothes to wear.*

It is during such devastating days in our lives that we encounter an unexpected intervention. Deus ex machina appears on the scene to give us a ray of hope. Wendell Shackelford, Director of Instructional Systems at HBJ Publishing Company, had interviewed me five months earlier. Out of the blue he phoned, offering me a position as editor of a curriculum that was part of a program to train minorities seeking employment. In addition to paying me fair pay for my services, Wendell offered me personal support and the gift of his friendship, both of which touched my heart. Since then and until the present time, our friendship is still going strong. It was his genuine emotional support and encouragement that made it possible for me to continue my courses and complete my education in the field of clinical psychology.

Faithful friends are lifesaving medicine, a sturdy shelter; whoever finds a friend has found a treasure. It was not a matter of chance that Wendell reached out for me and was eager to help me. It was God's divine intervention; it was a spiritual experience. As he offered help, I found myself growing in grace and wisdom. I learned to receive with gratitude and to give, share, love, and care. Caring for each other implied that our souls had connected to create a climate of reciprocity and concern for each other's wellness. We nurture our friendship and it continues to be vital between us.

Over the years, Wendell and I shared many experiences, mostly joyful ones. Benjamin Franklin once said, "A brother may not be a friend, but a friend will always be a brother." Wendell proved to be a good brother. I hope I have been a good brother for him.

My transition came gradually as I defined myself and worked on what I wanted in my life: more freedom, more energy, a decent way to make a living, and new goals. Adding three more years of training in psychology to my current master's degree in education, I was able to earn a doctorate degree. This helped me to make the transition more easily from the religious field to a different field, yet related to my theological background. I saw psychology as the study of the soul, especially the ailing soul that yearned for relief from the pain.

In letting go of the person I used to be, I found the new person I had become in my new situation. But as a new person, I had to reconcile myself with lingering past hurts. How else could I be an effective therapist who could bring harmony and peace to the lives of others if my life was still unsettled?

As I recollect my encounter with the hierarchy at that crucial time, I find myself no longer disappointed with the archbishop. As a spiritual shepherd, he had to be protective of his flock. Yet a part of me was reminded of Jesus who told the story of the good shepherd who would leave his flock and go in search of the lost sheep. At that time, I was the lost sheep, and I wanted the archbishop to reach out for me. He probably did not know how to handle my situation. I thought my story would have moved him with compassion, such as Jesus felt for his people. I visited the archbishop with the fantasy that he would extend support. I had the qualifications to work anonymously with the educational ministry of the archdiocese, and I would have been an asset to that department. The fact that he rejected me cannot be denied. At that time, he was probably caught unprepared to offer me a solution. As I look back, the problem had to do primarily with my naive expectations. Had I been in his position, perhaps I would have behaved in a similar way. Harboring an unforgiving spirit and entertaining negative feelings about him would have been a waste of energy and time. I needed to let go of my angry feelings and the expectations. Now my new challenge was to move on with my life. I believe that God forgives, but I had to let go of how I felt about the unkind reaction of my successor in the parish, above all let go of my negative thoughts about the archbishop's treatment of my case, and forgive myself for disappointing him, and anyone else.

Years later, I had the opportunity to visit the archbishop. When he saw me in my layman's clothes, he smiled and said, "I welcome the psychologist." This time, he was very receptive and invited me to stay for lunch. Cordially, he indicated that I should sit next to him. He introduced me to his personnel as Father Peter Kalellis, saying, "I call him Father because the priesthood is irrevocable. Once a priest, always a priest! Besides, he is also a wholesome and fulfilled man." Hearing his kind words, I replied gratefully, "Thank you, your Eminence." Now the archbishop seemed like a different man—humble and kind. *He must have gone through his own transformation,* I thought. He extended warm hospitality to me and jovially requested that I send him my latest books and visit him again. That day, when I returned home, Pat said, "You look happy; you're glowing. What happened?"

"It was a special visit," I said. "Simple reconciliation; I feel good about it."

The archbishop was a prolific writer, and I was pleased to know that he had read some of my writings, for he sent me a generous handwritten letter: "I feel joy and pride about your new direction in life. Truly, your ministry, which now includes the 'written word,' continues to be on target, helping the people of God. I noticed in one of your books, you called Saint Paul, the Apostle of Reconciliation. You have named him well because he had made it his mission in life to bring peace and reconciliation among nations. I pray for your good health and continued progress in writing." In recent years, when I wanted to write a book about spirituality, I asked the archbishop for his opinion. He sent me another handwritten personal letter. He suggested that in writing such a book, it would be helpful to consider the five major steps of spiritual growth which he named self-awareness, self-knowledge, self-acceptance, self-purification, and fervent prayer. "I trust that you are going to develop these steps carefully, as you pursue personal enlightenment from God, the Father of all lights."

His thoughtful advice proved to be encouraging and helped me to complete my book. He died while I was writing this, but he left a lasting lesson with me: I need to make a change or an ongoing adaptation to new experiences, to avoid judgments, and to readjust my thoughts that I may see the reality of any other human being with a positive attitude.

Strange and miraculous things happen as we reconcile ourselves to our past hurts, when we forgive others and forgive ourselves. God restores peace in our hearts, opens a new door, and
provides proper direction. We have more energy, feel healthier,
happier, and rewarded.

God opened a new door for me. I was in a position to set up
a private practice in individual psychotherapy, and in marriage
and family therapy, doing something that I had done for many
years as a priest in hearing confessions and counseling others.
Once I had grasped this concept, I attended to my clients who
had problems with professional help and sensitivity. I saw the
process as a paradox. *I, a divorced man who could not save my own
marriage, was trying to restore the marriage of others?* Why not? If all
my knowledge came from studying psychological books, it would
be only an intellectual treatment for divorce issues. However, in
my practice, I have discovered that the most effective treatment
for divorcing or divorced spouses is to combine psychology with
my own personal experience that included human emotions; and
also to understand the true nature of each divorce.

Parents who are painfully disturbed with the behavior of
their children need advice. It is not helpful to tell them: "It's your
fault that your children turned out to be what they are. You raised
them to act that way." Blaming them or making them feel more
guilty than they already feel is counterproductive. What they
need to know is that children are gifts from God. They are given
to us and it is our job to offer them a safe, loving place to grow,
to teach them to be good citizens, and to encourage them to be
self-reliant. They are guests and, like any stranger in our home,
they need our hospitality. They become our good friends, and
then leave us to continue on their personal journey. Sometimes
they bring us immense joy and sometimes immense sadness, even
pain. Eventually, children leave their parents for various reasons:
to study, to look for work, to marry, to join the community, or simply to become independent. It is the ultimate joy to see our children happy and independent. It is then that smiles and tears
blend with each other, and it is then that we realize *our* children
are not ours—they have been given to us to become a true gift to
others.

Most parents have a hard time letting go of children whom they have raised. It is understandable why it is hard to give children their freedom—especially in our times of corruption, exploitation, and violence; yet, reality signals that children need to mature, make their own choices, and find their own way.

To bring comfort to some of the disappointed or hurting parents, I often introduce Kahlil Gibran's poetic wisdom from his book, *The Prophet*:

> Your children are not your children.
> They are the sons and daughters of Life's longing for
>   itself.
> They come through you but not from you.
> And though they are with you yet they belong not to
>   you.
> You may give them your love but not your thoughts,
> For they have their own thoughts.
> You may house their bodies but not their souls,
> For their souls dwell in the house of tomorrow, which
>   you cannot visit, not even in your dreams.
> You may strive to be like them, but seek not to make
>   them like you,
> For life goes not backwards nor tarries with yesterday.

As I dealt with people's problems, I was able to recognize my own strengths and weaknesses. My clients looked upon me as the one who could help them. I saw in their eyes their eagerness, expecting me to resolve their conflicts. I felt the Holy Spirit working through me, and I gained the ability to respond to their needs with faith, confidence, and emotional availability. What I offered seemed to prove of value and benefit to them. In my heart, I knew I could not cure anyone, but at least I could provide an empathic environment where healing was possible. *God* cures; professional therapists provide only a healing process. I have always believed that the potential for healing exists within us, as long as we do not prevent it.

I could not be Jesus who performed miracles and gave his

112

life for these people, but I was able to share part of my life with them. I had to humble myself and serve my clients, not as a doctor with a PhD degree on the wall, but as another human whose heart could touch their ailing soul, their inner self.

The change in career intensified my energy, and I wanted to do more. I was offered an adjunct professorship at Seton Hall University, South Orange, New Jersey, in the Department of Counseling Psychology.

During my teaching position, I realized the power of the *written word.* Counseling was effective, but additional support was needed, and that could be attained through the written word. I felt a new dynamic within me. I wanted to write self-help books, such as the one I had written while going through my divorce and my leaving the church that my own clients and the general public could use for guidance and emotional support. In the last twenty-eight years, this ambition has been fulfilled many times, and I am grateful. Truly, it is a most rewarding experience.

Lessons I Have Learned

- When we reach a state in life where we feel a battle waging within, whether we should remain in the safety of our present life, even if it is miserable, or risk moving forward to a future that may not be as secure, it is time to pull back and process the purpose and consequences of our new direction. Compulsive behavior can prove troublesome if we are not sure where we are going.

- Two paths enable us to move toward a mature state of being: The first path entails a careful and sensitive journey inward, to discover who we really are. The second path is a careful and sensitive journey outward, to discover the real world that surrounds us. The journey within provides an awareness of our strengths and weaknesses. This awareness helps to harmonize the inner self and to continue the external journey with confidence.

- When we start the journey within—taking a sort of inner inventory—we discover areas that are sensitive, broken, not quite right. Memory takes over and reveals buried traumas or repressed feelings that suddenly cause pain and confusion. At best, we can offer compassion to our past and realize that we are vulnerable. Understanding that we cannot change the events of the past, we can see them as an unalterable reality that has sharpened our current awareness.

- Wishing to change people—family, mates, relatives, friends, employers, employees—so that we can feel comfortable in their presence, or so that we may like them, is a fantasy that can result in frustration and distance between myself and them. Acceptance of this reality paves the way for better interaction and improved communication with others. Of course, acceptance presupposes we have accepted our own human nature and our vulnerability. Then it becomes easier to accept others. The inference is that any change we might wish needs to start with ourselves.

- As we rediscover who we are and accept the *real* self within us, two things can happen: We can accept people around us as *they* are, without trying to change them. We can also avoid the feeling of being anyone's victim, if our expectations are realistic. By feeling respect and love for who *we* are, we can offer a loving presence to others and seek relationships that are healthy and loving.

- Life at times seems difficult but it is seldom catastrophic. When we accept our life and what we have with gratitude, and not focus on what we do not have, we gain peace of mind. Choosing our attitude each day can prove a blessing. When we become sensitive to our reality that we are not just physical but also spiritual, then we see ourselves as capable people making the right choices and living a better life.

114

Additional Thoughts

In doing the extraordinary, one meets with many obstacles. An external force opposes our intention, especially if it is good or personal. If our expectations center on doing the ordinary—just getting along, conforming to the status quo so we can be thought of as normal—we will resonate to ordinary frequencies and be compliant or complacent.

We will succeed in finding purposeful living when we synchronize our potential, as limited as it may be, with the abundant potential that exists in others. By believing and presenting our good intentions with patience, persistence, and prayer, we shall be able to attain the unattainable.

PART THREE
Arriving

12

New Freedom

Once we say "yes" in the midst of life's transitions, the seed of self-realization and personal fulfillment is planted, and a wise sort of waiting is all that is required of us. Our task is to find ways of permitting and enabling the seed to germinate and flower.   —Orlo Strunk, Jr.

As I look back through the reservoir of my memory, I see two major events that took place at this time in my life. One followed the other and added two significant dimensions to my life. I married again and became a father again. I married Pat, a younger woman, in whose presence and loving company I felt exuberant. The woman of my choice, besides being young and beautiful, had an exciting and creative spirit. Within me, I had a vision that she could be like a mirror for me; she would be able to reflect my best self and my worst self—a mirror that would not change or distort the image but one that would reflect the truth. I needed the experience of being loved unconditionally, although I knew that only God loves us unconditionally. I was sensitive to what my part should be in Pat's life: to be loving and lovable. Initially, I visualized a simple and meaningful life with her, but I also had doubts that I could make her happy. Isn't it the dream of every man to make his woman happy? Doesn't the heart of every woman have the same desire, to make her man happy?

During our courtship, we had long and deep dialogues; I felt the most terrible anguish of ambivalence I ever experienced in my adult life. *Am I doing the right thing?* With each conversation, our need for further communication increased. I responded with delight to the inflection in her voice, her laughter, her maturity despite being twenty-three years younger than I. My whole being was afire with inner joy, and I wanted to talk to her and be with her forever. Eventually I felt confidence in myself; I knew I could love her unconditionally, and I wanted to devote my life to bringing joy into our relationship. My relatives and well-intentioned friends were skeptical. "She's too young." "It's not going to work." "As you get older the romance will be over, and then…?"

Most of Pat's relatives did not approve of her relationship with me and totally disagreed with the idea that she and I could have a successful marriage. In spite of their objections, being self-reliant and unaffected by their opinions, Pat followed the dictates of her heart. The fact that I was older was not an obstacle for her. She genuinely loved me, and she wanted to be my wife and life-time companion.

Some of my priest colleagues said that I would miss the glory of the church and the excitement of being a spiritual leader. There was meaning and value in their comments, but I chose to do what I wanted, and I took on the responsibility. I still have periodic tinges of guilt for what happened, and I do miss the glamour of church ritual and the importance of being a spiritual leader, but I've never been happier. It was the best choice of my life.

On June 25, 1978, we got married and began to enjoy our new life together. My bride was busy with her work and with making a home for us. My new career was rewarding. My job involved helping people find peace and a healthy direction in life.

As Pat and I traveled locally and overseas, enjoying the spirit of togetherness, the normal desires of a woman surfaced.

"Are we ever going to have a child?" Pat asked, with evident yearning in her eyes.

Initially, I was unable to offer a positive answer. For a long while I thought seriously about the idea of a baby. I was already a father of three; my fatherhood destiny was fulfilled. How would my three children feel having another sibling? In essence, I did not want to get involved in raising another child. But how could I deprive the woman I loved genuinely and unconditionally from the experience of motherhood? It did not seem fair. *A woman without a child is like a barren tree,* I thought. I could not do that to Pat, whom I loved dearly. It would not be fair or prudent to let her be childless.

Other aspects of our life together blossomed. Pat was not just a pretty face; she also had a beautiful soul. Her nurturing of our relationship refreshed my soul daily, and we continued to grow spiritually as well. From the backdrop of vivid memories, scars of emotional hurts and insecurities, I discovered within me untapped resources of love and creativity. After a busy day at the office, I returned home, singing on the way, to find my bride waiting in anticipation of a pleasant evening. Sometimes we talked into the night, and at other times we sat opposite each other in silence, drinking a cup of herbal tea or sipping a glass of homemade wine. With this human experience of being loving and feeling loved, how could we not believe that God loved us abundantly?

We could not stretch out the honeymoon forever. There were realities in life we both needed to face. Time flew by with incredible speed. Two years went by as quickly as yesterday, and our love took on flesh and bones and became a person, making its station in our home.

On May 26, 1980, I drove Pat to the hospital, and in the delivery room, within a few agonizing hours, I witnessed the mystery of birth. With awe and ecstasy, I reached out to touch the emerging infant, a seven-pounds-and-four-ounces girl, wailing her lungs out. The nurse in charge said, "You may touch your baby." I did, and she wrapped her thread-thin fingers around my index finger. I melted. What psychic button she must have touched to make my whole world turn around, I could not tell! Instantly, I fell incurably in love with her. Love-stricken at first sight! Carefully, I carried this tiny creature and placed her close to Pat's neck. Separated during the process of birth, mother and daughter now reconnected, a time for bonding, an unwritten ritual. The wailing ceased immediately, and I saw Pat's sweet smile dispelling any anguish of labor pain. Her eyes had a tearful glitter, a grateful smile.

"This is my second harvest," I whispered as I kissed her perspiring forehead.

"Thank you for making me a Mommy," she replied, placing the baby against her cheek.

"You did the hard work," I said, caressing her head.

I observed the mother and child bonding, and my body shivered, electrified with loving emotions. How accurately the Bible describes human beings: "Yet you have made them a little lower than God, and crowned them with glory and honor" (Psalm 8:5). So, at the age of fifty-four, I became the father of Katina—named in honor of my stepmother. The whole experience put me in contact with the more nurturing parts of myself. As I held, fed, and cared for this helpless infant, I felt the feminine part in me and regained a sense of emotional contact with my mother, who probably cared for me in a similar way.

Katina grew into a gorgeous girl with big brown eyes and long brunette hair that curled over her shoulders. When Pat went back to teaching, I spent the morning hours looking after this charming child. Katina had a collection of adorable colorful dresses for school, and I drove my little princess there every morning. She looked like a perfect picture, and I thought I looked like a perfect father. Noticing my excitement with Katina, some of the mothers said, "This must be your granddaughter? She is so beautiful." Silently, I nodded.

I was near sixty, and I was not about to explain details concerning Katina, my younger and second daughter. Do looks or years really matter? Aren't we more than aging bodies? Does the heart ever get old? I looked at my Katina and kissed her rosy cheeks as we parted each morning. She would kiss me and say in the Greek language, *S'agapo poly yiassou.* And I would say, "I, too, love you much. Goodbye." The echo of her sweet voice would reverberate in my ears on my way to work.

Life took a joyful turn, and I soared high, feeling an expanding love igniting each move I made. Being an adjunct professor at Seton Hall University, I was invited by different organizations to conduct seminars on contemporary issues such as parenting, family-living skills, self-esteem, parents and teenagers, combating conflicts, sexuality, and other topics related to human development. Who could ever imagine that a barefoot village boy, who had grazed goats and picked olives to make a living, survived the yoke of Nazis for four years on a Greek island, journeyed to America, became a priest, and twenty-one years later, ended up becoming a psychotherapist, as well as a professor teaching courses in psychology at the graduate school of a university? The story astounds even me.

To add to my own experience of life and my research and preparation to teach graduate students, I translated my verbal knowledge into written works. Once my books appeared on the market, people who read them seriously sought my help for their personal or family difficulties. Clients from different walks of life came seeking solace and healing, and my practice increased. Some individuals suffered more than others, and at times I felt convinced that pain and suffering are unavoidable parts of life. I tried to discover meaning in the midst of their suffering.

As we take a serious look around us, we may observe that everyone out there is hurting: your neighbor, your best friend, your auto mechanic, your mail carrier, and your doctor all have hidden hurts that we don't know about, just as we have hurts that they don't know about. The family is our first source of our deepest love and also the source of our deepest hurts. Those closest to us hurt us the most, whether deliberately or not. And if we are no longer members of a family, we experience even a deeper hurt, that of loneliness.

For physical illness we have medical doctors, and in our times there is medicine for most diseases. Where do we go when we suffer psychologically or spiritually? Psychology provides all kinds of therapies for different mental issues. But when most of our mental problems are a result of ailing souls, then we turn to God. Whimpering like hurt children, we look up to the Father, and if we don't get an instant response, we resent him, and we get angry. No matter how good we are as Christians, sometimes we get angry, and in our vulnerable moments, we distance ourselves from God. We stop going to church. We give up hope and prayer, although deep down in our hearts we know that God is present in our lives. His love for us is unconditional, even when we feel unlovable.

As a seasoned therapist, I'm aware that I cannot provide a total cure for my clients who hurt, but I can pave the way for healing. It is the grace of God that provides the ultimate cure. At times, sensing my powerlessness to provide comfort, after the suffering or depressed client left my office, I fell on my knees and humbly prayed, asking the Healer of All Pain to help.

Caught up in a whirlpool of psychological problems, I felt good in helping clients, whose troubles came in all varieties. It would take volumes to describe even a few of the situations that I encountered. I had to refer severely depressed or suicidal clients to a psychiatrist who, besides giving a diagnosis, could prescribe medication. Most of us know that troublesome situations, suffering, and pain are inevitable parts of life. There is no escape from the realities of our fragile and vulnerable human condition. How each one of us faces reality is the challenge of our maturing process. We may not have easy solutions to difficult problems, yet we are aware that solutions exist. When a person has a true desire to solve a lingering problem yet is unable to find a viable solution, seeking professional help is imperative. It would take a number of books to describe the variety of psychological issues that clients bring to mental health specialists.

As I write this chapter, an unusual and scary story knocks at the door of my memory. It happened several years ago, but I still remember the impact that it had on my career. A disturbed adolescent, whom we shall call David, had impulse control issues. In school he had excelled as an A student, but a time came when he refused to do any schoolwork. He rapidly failed and joined other dropouts who were involved in villainy. His high-school guidance counselor suggested that he seek therapy.

One rainy afternoon, David entered my office carrying a violin case containing a gun equipped with a silencer. He told me about himself. He was determined to kill his parents, a couple of teachers, and himself. "I want to clean up the scum in my school," he said. Angrily gesturing with his fingers, he pressed a pretend pistol against his temple.

I was in a quandary as to what kind of therapeutic intervention I should follow. I must admit I was scared. I told David what happened during my teenage years: how the Nazis had invaded

my village, ransacked our house, pointed a gun at me, shot innocent people, and starved others to death.

In school, David had learned about the Holocaust. He knew
nothing about the rest of Europe or the total of fifty-seven million
people who died during World War II. He could not believe that
the Nazis had invaded the mainland of Greece, as well as my
small island and my small village of Moria. My experiences made
an impression on him; I could see compassion in his big brown
eyes. When David heard the gruesome details, his response was,
"Wow! All that, and I'm complaining! How did you survive?"

"We were under Nazi occupation for four years, and during
that time, three of my friends and I endured hunger, beatings,
and fear of being killed. We loved each other and believed in
God who kept us alive. We attended church regularly, and tried
to help people who were hungry or sick."

David offered more information about himself. His parents
were going through an ugly divorce, and hearing them tearing
into each other violently, he felt that he was the cause of their
quarrels. He felt responsible. "If I were not here, they would
probably stay together," he said.

"Divorce is an adult issue, and children pay a high price
when their parents break up," I said.

It took weeks before David could understand that he did not
cause the divorce, that it was not his fault that the marriage of his
parents fell apart, and that he was carrying unnecessary guilt for
something that was not his responsibility.

"You are caught in the web of a painful family issue," I said.
"You don't have to use painful means to fix it. You know your parents love you; now you need to endure a period of discomfort
and readjustment."

"Like you endured the Nazis," he said sadly.

"Something like that," I said. "Once you accept the reality
that your parents will no longer live together, then you will
focus on what *you* can do to feel better, on what seems important
to *you*."

Having heard my story and noticing my interest in his situation, David gained enough trust to tell me more about how he felt
and about his current activities. He had strong artistic talents—

I still have some of his artwork in my file. His life took a turn for the better. He found interest in his friends and in his art; he was pleased with my encouraging words. He continued his therapy, and with each weekly session I sensed an improvement in his attitude. It took two years before he became aware of the reality of his life and his future as a male. He asked me to dispose of his gun in a confidential way. I was happy to oblige.

Any seasoned therapist, someone who appreciated David's confusion, could have helped him and pointed out a path for him to follow. David could have endured his situation better, perhaps, if he had realized that the pain he was experiencing was the natural result of the ending process of home security, and that he was entering the ground of an insecure future, a future that required planning. He would have felt less angry had he realized how common his experience was. Then he would have been able to face his dilemma more confidently.

David felt his mother was to blame for not holding on to his father; he had to let go of his anger toward her. He ceased asking, *Why divorce?* He realized that his mother loved him and that her love was a blessing and that it enabled him to move on with his life. He knew that his father loved him too and that his caring was genuine. At the same time, David was angry with his father for not sustaining a home for him. He appreciated his father's generous gesture to pay school tuition; David thanked him but decided to get a job and pay for his own education. His father did not argue the point, thinking it was wise to allow David to walk alone the unmapped world and become a self-reliant man.

Beyond parental love and support, David had to find the path that enabled him to become his own man, a sort of inner mating with the world outside of the warmth and security of the family nest. David gradually found the path, and today he is married and is busy at work in his New York office, where he enjoys a reputation as an excellent commercial artist.

Lessons I Have Learned

- When we make a decision with confidence in ourselves and with the attitude that we will be responsible for the results of our decision, nothing external can influence our choice. Timing and the state of mind are crucial for making decisions. However, under intense emotions such as anger, deep grief, depression, or any caused by a traumatic event, it is not wise to make and follow through a major decision.

- "Make haste slowly" is an ancient axiom that I used earlier and that applies here as well. We should not rush into anything without carefully considering the consequences of our decision. A decision should not be absolute. If the decision causes a negative effect, the decision-maker ought to be able to change it or consult a reliable source for direction.

- If a marriage is failing, professional help is necessary. When partners reach an impasse and no longer want to live together, divorcing and marrying again does not guarantee happiness. However promising the new relationship may seem, we need to examine ourselves before committing ourselves to a second marriage. A self-inventory may help us see what is in us that contributes to our happiness or misery.

- Advanced technology and life's constant changes throw us off balance and cause emotional insecurities. It is essential for men and women to look into themselves and develop new coping skills to face reality. It is important to choose personal priorities and spend time relaxing and enjoying life, avoiding external influences that cause trouble.

- Once we begin to understand the essence of our being, not simply the physical self but the invisible self, we must learn to examine our perceptions. Then, by removing certain major obstacles that stifle our well-being, we will be better equipped to move on with life and live with greater self-confidence.

- The way we view ourselves determines, in large part, how we think, how we feel, and how we act. Humans are endowed with complex and contradictory attitudes. They can love or hate, build or destroy, be kind or cruel, generous or greedy. They have freedom to make choices. God gives life, but it is our challenge and responsibility to design it.

Additional Thoughts

Sad endings signal new beginnings. The sadness causes emotional pain and passivity. A new beginning for one who is compelled by circumstances to change, or who is willing to make a new beginning for personal reasons, is full of surprises—causing ambivalence, doubt, insecurity, and eventually a decision to move forward. Looking back to yesterday, we may suffer the destiny of Lot's wife, as referred to in the Bible. She was told to leave Sodom and Gomorrah and not look back. But she did look back and instantly turned into a pillar of salt. A pillar of salt may have strength, but it has no life.

The implication here is that when we abide by what has happened to us in the past, we become passive, we become victims of the past, and consequently we have no strength to make a new beginning.

13

Feeling Good about Yourself

Adversities, pain, suffering are parts of life primarily caused by how we live, think, feel, and react. To combat these a change is necessary, and change implies a choice to change thoughts and behavior. Since we are what we believe, think, and do, if we want to change what we are, we must undertake a new mode of life.
—Allen Wheelis

At this point in my life, my future as a therapist was clearly defined. I had to focus on helping people whose life was emotionally troubled. Since childhood, it was in my nature to help my family and improvise for others who needed help. In helping others I felt loved and connected with them. Doing the smallest favor for someone gave me a wonderful feeling inside. In my adult years, when I became a priest, I once again found myself connecting with people as if they were my family. Being available and sensitive to their needs, I offered spiritual guidance and emotional support, and shared with them my understanding of Christ, his love, and his compassion.

In my later life, when I chose psychotherapy, another issue needed serious attention. *How could I help others without getting entangled in their problems?* Were I to become too emotionally involved, I would become part of their problem, and then I would be unable to be effective in their lives. I am grateful to my experienced supervisors—psychiatrists, psychologists, and family therapists—who demonstrated and taught me the techniques of psychotherapy. They reminded me of the Hippocratic axiom:

"Physician, heal thyself!" I needed to pull myself together, become a whole person, and feel emotionally sound. It took me several years of personal therapy, group therapy, and sensitive supervision by knowledgeable professionals who helped me to recover my senses.

Most people in conflict or emotional trouble have high expectations of their therapists or of themselves. When their world falls apart, clients need to have answers. In time of pain or discomfort, they look for relief. During periods of intense pain, they believe that they are the only ones in the world who are experiencing such suffering. It is hard for them to see that certain painful issues, such as trouble in relationships, unmet personal needs, or dissatisfactions, are common results of how people perceive life, and what they decide to do about it. No one likes adversity, pain, or tragedy, but they are part of life. We do not particularly like it, but trouble, the uninvited guest, visits all of us from time to time.

Major crises—such as illness, death of a loved one, divorce, a sudden break in a relationship, loss of a promising job, not getting the promotion we expected, or any other important issue—raise disturbing questions in our minds. Uncomfortable about our personal situation, about who we are, or where we are in each junction of life, we blame or project our dissatisfactions on to other people or other things. We react with anger to people who expect us to be different from who we really are. Listening to their opinions or wrong perceptions of us can trigger only more anger and frustration. We are troubled, not because of what happens around us, but because of what happens within us. Most of us may not be aware how our soul suffers if we live a superficial life.

Succumbing to despair or emptiness, some people grope in a dark alley looking for a possible rescuer or a miracle-working therapist to help them. When I notice a client's emotional breakdown, I want to stretch out my arms, embrace the person, and relieve the pain. Such a fantasy might provide comfort for the moment, but it does not solve the problem. I have learned that the best treatment I can provide is to be honest from the start. When a troubled client comes to my office, I make it clear that I am not a miracle-worker. I say with a smile, "I do not operate a

130

spa where people go for a massage and other relaxing experiences that provide a physical tune-up for a couple of days, but I promise to work and wrestle along with you in combating your problem and finding a realistic solution."

Most of my clients seem to accept my approach. Fortunately, in our times there are solutions for most problems; of course, the suffering person needs to be willing to take responsibility and participate in the solution. Therapy is costly. It takes money, time, and energy, and it requires an earnest desire to seek solutions. On an average day, a therapist may deal with clients who face personal or relationship problems, hate or rage, unresolved traumas of the past, inability to let go of emotional hurts, conflicts, impasses, unfinished business. These clients are in search of viable answers for survival or coping mechanisms to assist them through difficult times. Some of them know what needs to be done, but they doubt their own capabilities.

Most professionals in the healing arts offer a sense of understanding and empathy; they become the mirrors in which their clients can see who they really are and what the truth is about them. Possible options or suggestions, given in an empathic and warm environment, promote clients' interest in therapy, allow them the opportunity, and encourage their responsibility to choose what seems to work for them. An experienced and seasoned therapist can be of great help.

The process may be long and tedious, and it requires a positive attitude. Another word that gets at the heart of therapy is *change*. We need to change our negative thoughts—refrain from blaming and judging others, and stop harboring anger, frustration, rage, resentment, or guilt about the wrongs of life—and start to repair our self. All past hurts and wrongs exist only in the mind. They cannot be touched or changed. By fostering or reminding ourselves of negative experiences, we continue to feel emotionally upset. A negative attitude or distorted thinking diminishes our vitality, affects us emotionally, and distances us from healthy relationships. Negativity shows in our voice, eyes, face, and physical demeanor. As a result, many people avoid our company. Choosing to focus only on the negative causes depressed feelings and anxiety. However, choosing to focus always on the positive and not dealing with the negative is equally harmful and unrealistic. Each one of us has to find a balance between the positive and the negative situations of life.

Here are questions that merit our attention: Do people really change? Can we really change our attitude? I have seen a large number of people who made dramatic changes in their lives and found fulfillment in their new lifestyle. I have also had disappointments. Some people, in spite of the time and money they invested in therapy, went back to the unhappy, miserable lifestyle familiar to them. They resisted the therapeutic experience, and they made no attempt to consider another option as an alternate approach to life. I recall several classic examples:

After a couple of sessions, some clients have said, "I'm okay now. I don't think I need more therapy. I do have a handle on things now. I'm fine."

Others have said, "My insurance does not cover therapy and I cannot afford to pay you" or—

"I know you are good, but I don't have much money; besides I have no time; I'm dealing with a tough schedule at work."

And still others: "I'm not going to change."

"My intimate other doesn't want to change."

"Things don't change."

Some of the excuses may have been genuine, but within most lurks what every therapist encounters, *resistance* to possible adjustment. To such responses, I suggest the concept of mature and responsible thinking.

I simply say, "Perhaps it is not a change of character you are looking for, because your character is already formed. This is what you believe about yourself, so this is who you are now. How about feeling better? Mature thinking and behavior, responsibility, and responsible action may improve your situation. This could be a realistic and more rewarding goal to pursue."

A question worthy of consideration is, What brings people to therapy? During my thirty-five years of practice, I have often asked that question. Obviously clients do not come to tell me how happy they are. They come because a nagging issue is disturbing their daily life. The issue may produce one or more of the following symptoms: anxiety, boredom, conflict, depression, lack of direction or fulfillment in life, emotional fatigue, a sense of emptiness, or insecurity. When we interpret our own symptoms like these in a negative manner, we disturb our inner peace and our hope for happiness. Truly, it is hard to see what part we play in our current life that makes us unhappy. A brief dialogue may clarify what may be going on in an unhappy person's life:

THERAPIST:	Are you doing something that may be contributing to your unhappiness?
CLIENT:	I don't think so. Why would I make myself miserable?
THERAPIST:	Perhaps something may be going on that makes you unhappy.
CLIENT:	I don't know what that could be.
THERAPIST:	You made an appointment to see me. Why?
CLIENT:	I thought you may be able to help me...
THERAPIST:	What kind of help do you think you may need?
CLIENT:	I don't know.

Understandably the first visit to a therapist's office may be intimidating. Sometimes, under the presenting problem, another more-serious problem may be revealed. Clients usually respond according to how they perceive their situation, how they feel in a therapist's office, and how far they are able to trust the therapist. Initially, they may blame other people or other things for their misery. Some clients feel they are victims of circumstances. They blame their upbringing, physical abuse, bad parenting—the list can be long. They believe in the excuse that what happens in their life now is not really their fault.

People who think life owes them something—"I am a good human being, I don't bother anyone, I deserve happiness, I expect to be treated well"—always blame others for their own unhappiness, failures, or tough times. How often do we hear: "My mother annoys me." "I like my work, but I hate my boss; he

133

expects too much of me." "I do not talk to my sister; she is too selfish." "My dad is a controlling man." Drawbacks occur as part of the overall life experience.

Apart from incurable illness, amputation, or defective genes, a person who feels victimized, a *victim*, by nature of his or her perceptions, tries to discover or invent somebody to blame, a *victimizer*. The victimizer may be a tough parent, a bad government, a demanding employer, a dysfunctional family, an uncaring spouse, an insensitive friend, or a cold God. It seems that once a victimizer is defined, the victim feels relief.

Yet, as long as we view adversities unrealistically, think of ourselves as victims, and try to blame the victimizer who causes our unhappiness, we will continue to live a life of fear and anxiety. It is of greater benefit to transcend the causes of our unhappy feelings and do whatever we can to alleviate our problems. We can search for and pursue possible solutions on all levels: individual, familial, societal, and global. Then the blaming may end, and if the client continues in therapy, the search for solutions becomes a challenge, a choice, and a promise.

Most Americans believe that the world is basically a nice place. It is. Life is mostly fair, and we are good people who deserve to have good things, which we work to attain. Such beliefs can play an important role toward leading a happier and healthier life. But we cannot live mesmerized by a mythology of complacency and power that our system is invincible and that we cannot be deprived.

Our technology is responsible for the general level of physical comfort in Western society. In recent years, mass media, instant communication systems, digital cameras, computers, cellular phones, e-mails, and so forth have become part of everyday living. As a result, the needs of other nations and of less fortunate people become invisible. When we read of their sad conditions, we look upon their situation as a sign of someone's failure; we blame their government system and dismiss the tragic information as an infringement on our right to happiness. It is a sad commentary on our speeches about caring for the needs of others.

Should an adversity occur to us, it is difficult for us to return to happier living. No normal human being is content to put up with pain and suffering. Even a minor accident or trauma can have emotional impact, and we begin to doubt our capability to endure other adverse circumstances, face reality, and move on with life. Personally, I grew up with few of life's luxuries, however, I have had the good fortune of visiting other countries, including the Middle East, Turkey, Africa, and Greece. I have arrived at my own personal perceptions. Pain and suffering are experienced by all human beings; and in certain parts of the world, natural catastrophes as well. I have observed that people in other nations appear to have a greater acceptance and tolerance. Part of this may be due to their belief system, or it may be that suffering is more familiar and more visible to people in underdeveloped nations.

We have much of the good things of life—abundance of food on the table, medical and dental care, decent clothing, conveniences, and endless opportunities for any aspiring person— but now we are forced to acknowledge our vulnerability. We need to wake up from the American dream and realize that the yesteryear Vietnam War, subsequent small wars, the current conflict in the Middle East, the continuous threat of terrorism, domestic corruption, the high cost of living, and exploitation have tarnished our image of living in the ideal nation. With a great dose of humility, we need to think seriously and accept the reality about who we are as a nation, and what each one of us can do for the other, for our homes and our country.

In view of where we live and the opportunities available to each one of us, why are we so unhappy? We do not want to admit that because of the spectacular advancement of science, our pride about it, and the desire to attain the most recent gadgets that clever advertisement brings to our attention, we have created for ourselves a status anxiety, a stress epidemic that puts our lives in danger.

Instead of feeling complacent or comparing life in America with life in other nations, we should be grateful for our bounty, and try to nurture a spirit of compassion and charity for the needs of others. A great start for a new era would be to bring God back into our homes and our schools. Think of God as the Giver of All Blessings. His gifts to us—every breathing moment, every heartbeat, the glory of nature and of the universe, and every step we take—are an expression of his love. Is it difficult to offer prayers of gratitude to God in whose world we live? As we learn to love God with our heart and believe that he cares for us, then we might want to share this joyful feeling with our neighbor. But if we ignore his presence, we continue a purposeless, empty life. Suppose someone doubts or does not believe in the existence of God. A prayer, even by an atheist or a skeptic, could be of benefit: *Oh God, I do not know if you exist, but if you do, help me to find you. Amen.*

Of course, every human being wishes and strives to be free of suffering. To attain a sense of inner joy and happiness would be a valuable goal to pursue. In *Benefits of Happiness*, psychologist Rich Bayer writes: "Happiness is good for us. It brings us physical, mental, and emotional health....People who are happy do better in social relationships, use their intelligence more efficiently, are more optimistic, have better physical health, [and] are more creative. Happy people tend to be kinder to others and to express empathy more easily."

In view of what I have experienced, learned, and studied as a psychotherapist, I prefer to offer my clients hope and optimism and help them realize that there is something more than what they see in the mirror. Thoughts and feelings are the invisible parts in charge of our life. The physical self can be touched, contained, nourished, and protected. We are aware that the body ages, changes, and eventually returns to its elements, back to earth. The spiritual part that keeps the body alive lives on. That part nurtures innate virtues of kindness, love, compassion, and forgiveness, which forever grow but never die. They emit inner peace and joy. Would it be to our benefit to maintain a negative or bitter attitude? When we remove the letter *i* from the word *bitter,* and replace it with the letter *e, bitter* becomes *better.* If you happen to be bitter about anything or anyone, try to remove the *i* for one or two weeks. You may notice the difference in how you feel.

Think for a moment: Are we happy with the way our life has evolved? If we are honest, we can easily answer, *not really.* Happiness is an inner emotion, and when we expect to find it outside of ourselves through material accumulations, we are disappointed. The more we bring into our lives, the more things we want to buy and own. The addiction to *more* of everything seems to have no limits—*more* stimulating experiences, *more* success in earning *more* money, and *more* status symbols. Imitating others, or wanting what others have that we do not, prevents even the joy of small things.

Lessons I Have Learned

- In a world that seems out of control, we take charge and have some control over our lives. It is possible to monitor our perceptions; to control our thoughts, our words, and our social situations; and to refine our recreations and improve our physical environment. We cannot dictate how other people should live. They are entitled to design their own life. We are also entitled to design or redesign ours.

- Living without encountering adverse or negative situations is rare and not realistic. Disappointments, frustrations, misunderstandings, anger, deprivation feelings of being taken advantage of—these aspects of life and how we perceive them disturb our peace and happiness. We can choose to do something about it.

- Having heightened or unrealistic expectations, or trying to live like others we admire and whom we think of as most fortunate, makes happiness elusive. We do not really know the unseen part of the rich and famous. We see only appearances, or what mass medias bring to our attention.

- In a country where an abundance of goods are available, we have no worries about survival needs. In other parts of the world, people are simply content to have a job, buy food, raise a family, and live in peace. Happiness is not their priority, survival is their major concern.

- Our search for happiness requires respect, truth, forgiveness, joy, and peace, which are essentially states of mind. As our thoughts generate feelings, we need to be aware of what we think. We don't have to carry mental baggage. We have enough experience to recognize what are good and positive thoughts, and what is distorted or negative thinking. As we refine the way we think, we gain peace and power to avoid problems.

- St. Paul offers words of wisdom: "Finally, beloved, whatever is true, whatever is honorable, whatever is just, whatever is pure, whatever is pleasing, whatever is commendable, if there is any excellence and if there is anything worthy of praise, think about these things" (Phil 4:8). His brief admonition truly provides a basic step toward a happier and more rewarding life.

Additional Thoughts

Suffering is imposed externally or internally, and it seems there is no escape. It may be impersonal and unavoidable, caused by fire, flood, hurricane, earthquake, cancer; or it may be man-made, caused by accidents, divorce, war, and rape. Some people suffer emotionally because of either bad choices or distorted perceptions. They greet, glitter, and smile, and show nothing of the misery inside. Only they know their despair. In some cases, the traumas are so deep and painful that the suffering people cannot see the potential of getting well.

Do victims have a choice? Is there a little corner of relief? Perhaps victims of pain may bow in prayer and turn to Jesus, the God of suffering, or they may curse and throw spears at the supposed enemy. They have a choice: to pursue healing or to allow suffering to continue.

14

Becoming Better

There is a strange lightness in the heart when one accepts the aging aspect of life in good faith. How pleasant is the day when we give up striving to be young and slender. "Thank God!" we say, "those illusions are gone."

—Alain de Botton

Celebrating my sixty-fourth year and feeling a tinge of sadness that seven more years had gone by, I sat alone by a window overlooking my wife's colorful garden. Peonies, petunias, daisies, lilacs, color, beauty, and fragrance refreshed my spirit. I kept thinking that flowers are like humans; they serve their purpose, wither away, and die. I walked over to our dining area and looked at myself in a mirror on the wall. My eyes rested on my hands, a mosaic of brown liver spots. I pinched my skin, and it took a long time to return back to its former shape. "I'm slowly withering away," I whispered to myself.

Aging is an inevitable reality. Every day that passes, we are reminded that we are getting older, and some day we are going to die. Woody Allen's humor evoked a smile: "I don't mind dying. I just don't want to be there when it happens." Well, as *I* get older, I *do* mind dying. I want to live.

Not many of us want to age or die. Most of us would like to remain youthful or to look younger. We indulge in all sorts of techniques to remove our wrinkles and layers of fat; mass media encourages us and helps us accomplish our goal. Colorful magazines, TV advertisements, and radio announcements inundate our minds to convince us to overcome our physical defects; they present us with a selection of spas, exercise facilities, elixirs, vitamins, and potions—anything our heart desires that will give us a better, happier, and longer life.

Without serious thoughts about life and appreciation for what is *now* available to us, and without self-confidence in our human potential, aging can become a constant source of anxiety. Such anxiety and worry exacerbate the defects that accompany the aging process. I am not suggesting that taking vitamins, exercising, and caring for our health are not of any value. They are important, and in many cases, they delay the coming of wrinkles and sagging. Civilization and science have contributed a great deal to human longevity. Yet diets, cosmetic surgery, or accumulation of material wealth will not stop the aging process. By maintaining a positive attitude, valuing our own wisdom, and appreciating what we have available in the present, we can age gracefully and live longer.

We live in a time that denies death and distorts the dying experience. We need a new vision of maturity and longevity. We do not have to be victims of aging or dying; we should not permit either of these two inevitable processes to victimize us. Death has no dominion over life; God does. Children and young adults do not think about aging. They don't invest time worrying about getting old. Older people do. They sense it, they see it, they feel it. Aging is not an accident. It is a natural phenomenon. All living creations age and eventually die.

Our heart whispers that this great marathon called life, which started at birth, cannot go on forever. If we accept the sunrise, we need to realize and understand that there is a sunset. Growing older is part of life. Blossoms and flowers wither and die. Trees get old, rot, and decay. The whole world gets old. Only one remains immortal: the Grim Reaper never gets old.

Our bodies know about aging, and at some point in our lives, the body is totally committed to these late stages. With moderate care, the body can sustain itself well, and age gracefully. Our concern about aging and the fear of not being able to function as younger people cause anxiety. Mass media usually portrays elders as either senile, doddering, ineffectual buffoons or as wholesome, unwrinkled, white-haired fun-seekers who work hard to recapture the vigor of their middle years so that they can keep up with the youth culture.

Most advertisements do not portray older people who have come to terms with the facts of physical aging and psychological maturity; rather they portray idealized older people who can still compete athletically, sexually, and financially with the younger generation. Every week I receive one or two magazines in full color, pointing out the glories of longevity, truly good and encouraging material. I am also happy to see a number of inspirational publications that can help us nurture our souls, and enable us to become better people.

A study of the type of characters who appeared during one week on prime time television indicates that out of 464 role portrayals, only seven appeared to be over sixty-four years of age. Out of one hundred commercials, only two involved older characters. But older folks are not always ignored; a few years ago we were depicted in films such as *On Golden Pond, Cocoon,* and *Fried Green Tomatoes,* which displayed sympathetic portrayals of older people's real-life struggles.

When we accept aging as a natural unfolding of life, it is easier to stop worrying about slowing down and diminishing strengths. We sense the difficulty of getting out of bed in the morning. We feel the aching in the joints, and we accept these physical changes. Accepting them does not mean that we give up. Giving up means resigning ourselves to a declining life and having no joy, love, or hope for the present day and the immediate tomorrow.

While our body ages and different parts of our body lose their strength and vitality, we have a heart that is ageless. I am not referring to the physical organ that pumps blood into our body. I am talking about the inner self, the spiritual part that deserves respect and honor. It is the spiritual self that synthesizes wisdom from the experiences of a long life and makes it available to the coming generations.

Denial of aging causes depressing feelings; negative thoughts about aging are an affliction. Ideas about the young and our culture of youth can make the aging process morbid, and it disguises the truth about the elderly. At the present time, most of our art focuses on youth and middle age. Aging has never been a significant cultural force. Yet, as elder art grows in popularity and influence, young people will be exposed to images of older people that stress inner beauty, purpose, radiance, and distilled wisdom. Rather than experiencing the horror of growing old, we can begin anticipating elderhood as the summit of life.

The label *senior citizen* was an invention of young adults; it confined the aging population to a category considered worthless. Let's not get stuck with the label *senior citizen*. We are not just senior citizens who get gold watches upon retirement, move to Sun Belt states, and play cards, shuffleboard, and bingo ad nauseam. We are not wrinkled babies, succumbing to a trivial, purposeless waste of our later years. Let's not visualize ourselves in bare nursing homes, cared for by irritable nurses—mad, mute, and smelly, waiting for death. Then, aging would not seem as an irretractable affliction.

What are we? We are elders, the wisdom-keepers who have an ongoing responsibility for maintaining society's well-being and safeguarding the health of our ailing planet. Elderhood is a time to rediscover inner richness for self-development and spiritual growth. It is also a time of transition and preparation for dying, which is at least as important as preparing for a career or family.

Of course, human aging is an activity of the soul. In our times, human life extends; people live to be sixty, seventy, eighty, ninety, and now we have a large group of centenarians. Beyond muscular usefulness and sensory acuteness, humans meditate on recliners, march on the treadmill, or write their memoirs.

Full awareness of our aging implies that we have come to terms with our past. It is of great significance to reflect on the wealth of our experiences—our personal achievements as well as our unresolved conflicts. In an attempt to understand what our life has meant thus far, we can visualize it as a kind of "inner cooking or brewing." Think of the flame as our knowledge of mortality. The ingredients are a lifetime of perceptions, experiences, and relationships as yet not finalized, and the vessel is our heart.

In some cases, becoming reacquainted with the past involves pain. Understandably, we do not want to reopen old wounds, but as we become more spiritual, we can reach back into the past with a spirit of humility. We can repair events and relationships that we perceive as failures and disappointments.

Although we live in the present time, a part of ourselves is imprisoned in the pain of past relationships where incomplete experiences cry out to be healed. Although years ago we may have left home and its early life traumas, the wounded inner-child still weeps within us. By doing the work of inner repair, we can release ourselves from the prison-bound self of a former time. We can also forgive ourselves for the pain that we caused to others. We can learn to revisit the joys and sorrows of our lives and say yes to them for the pearls of wisdom they imparted.

When we courageously confront the past, we discover how much we have gained from apparent losses or failures. Most of us have unhealed emotional scar tissue that keeps our hearts closed and defensive. We need to open our hearts, learn to let go, and allow healing to take place.

What happens when we instead hold onto resentment and angry feelings? In our daily life, we carry the resentment wherever we go and in whatever we do. As we go to work, our anger is with us and invades our activities. We sit down to eat with resentment as our companion. We try to sleep, and our offender keeps us awake. During the night, the ugly resentment haunts us.

What are our choices? We can either continue holding onto our past with all its resentments and hostile feelings and be miserable, or we can let go and forgive the injustices we suffered and thereby liberate ourselves from the tyranny of our past. Once we start practicing forgiveness, we will experience new strength and new vitality that will enable us to involve ourselves in acts of charity and love. We will see the world with different eyes. Beyond any doubt, we will totally enjoy what remains of our life.

This much we can say with confidence: all humans need additional years for a unique purpose—to *refine* our character and to grow better, not just older. The Giver of All Life knows that, and he will grant us the needed time to make amends, restore relationships, and refine our being. In our older years, some of us may suffer mentally, physically, or emotionally; some of us may feel that death is around the corner; some will feel that we still have a few good years ahead. We need to bring into our lives the concept of refinement, a sort of inner cleansing. We need to purify our soul by letting go of the wrong done to us and possibly amend the wrongs we did to others.

A wise statement by Thomas Moore in his book *Care of the Soul*, strikes a chord in my heart: "Curing implies the end of trouble; you don't have to worry about whatever was or is bothering you any longer. But caring has an ongoing attention. Conflicts may never be fully resolved. Your character will never change radically, although it may go through some interesting transformation."

It is our human destiny to go through personal transformation. From childhood through adulthood to old age, we go through many physical changes. At the same time, something special and good is growing inside us. We need to give it proper sunshine and nourishment to insure that it grows to full health and vigor. Meanwhile, we live in a state of tension between two realities: First, the world endangers our existence, tempting us with hopes of happiness and demanding our obedience and conformity to its rules. Second, we are aware of the supernatural existence of God for whom, even unknowingly, we yearn; this Divine Being calls us forth beyond the laws and boundaries of our life that starts here on earth and continues in God's eternal kingdom.

If any changes are to occur in our afflicted world, each one of us will have to respond to life in a spirit of humility and kindness. The *me, myself,* and *I* perception will have to be modified to include others who face the aging process, who have needs and deserve a decent life. The attitude changes and becomes *other-centered*, which promotes caring for others. We must keep our hearts open and become more accepting, benevolent, generous, and compassionate. The realization and sadness we feel because we cannot live forever helps us start seeing our brief journey as a preparation for our eternal life.

Lessons I Have Learned

- Aging is unavoidable, but we can grace it with imaginative ideas and protect it from negative thoughts. We can keep our mind active and our body moving.

Above all, we must let go of bad memories and negative experiences. We must rediscover ways to live better. We need to allow the spirit within guide us and help us soar higher than human weakness.

- There is a degree of irritability that many older people experience. Everything seems to bother them: "The weather is too hot or too cold...Things are not as they used to be...Goods have gone up in price...The world is in turmoil...Today's youth are unruly...Politicians are dishonest...The government is not caring for the elderly...Social security is not enough to live on." The list of negatives is endless. Scarcely any changes can be accomplished if we focus on these irritating issues. We may voice our opinion as long as we do not obsess about it.

- A positive attitude is important. We can be ageless as we make certain changes to better our life. When we honestly know and accept who we are—physically, mentally, emotionally, and spiritually—we can focus on something we always wanted to do. Even one single motivation can make our journey to aging more rewarding and more peaceful.

- If we think of pains, aches, wrinkles, appearances, and activities we can no longer do, it will make us miserably unhappy. If we commiserate with others, we feel frustrated. When we compare ourselves with others who seemingly enjoy life or who have conveniences that we do not have, then we definitely create misery.

- A healthier approach to aging is to develop an attitude of gratitude. We can spend grateful moments thinking of what we have, rather than what we do not have. A grateful attitude is the realization that parts of our life are immortal. The wisdom we have gained over the years; the love we have shared; the humility, sincerity, kindness, and generosity we have shown—these virtues never die. They live on in the hearts of people who follow us.

- As the sun moves toward sunset each day, we can visualize the sunrise. We can plan to enjoy tomorrow as if it were our last day on earth. If we have sons or daughters, we can give them a call or plan a visit. If there are grandchildren, we can think of hugging them, telling them a story, or listening to their innocent sounds. Their toys, songs, and play can be revitalizing.

Additional Thoughts

When we get out of bed every morning, we usually look at our physical appearance in the mirror. That's all we see, a body that ages and changes. As we pause, we realize that our body, as far back as we can remember, went through many other bodies—the baby, child, teenager, young adult, middle age, golden age. What has not changed is our unseen part, our spiritual dimension, our soul, the part that never dies. That part contains virtues that we can use until our last breath—faith, hope, love, justice, and kindness. Instead of worrying about our lack of energy, or our failing memory, or our lack of ability to do things we used to do, it would be better to focus on what we have—confidence, experience, knowledge, wisdom. When we value what we have, we might then be able to persuade ourselves that we don't really get older, we get better.

15

Hacuna Matata

*The more that I hear about human suffering the more I believe
I can respond with a sign of hope. The forces of darkness cannot pull me into despair and make me one more of their many
victims. Those who struggle for survival deserve our attention.*
—Henri J. M. Nouwen

Hacuna Matata are the three words my family heard again
and again while we were in Africa. *Hacuna Matata* means "Do not
worry about anything." It was a philosophy alien to me. However,
my experiences in Africa have given me some understanding of
how such a philosophy is necessary for survival for those living in
conditions of deprivation.

The great land of Africa attracts people for different reasons: enterprising company executives want the wealth that can
come from exploitation; politicians pursue their own personal
interests; adventurers go on exploration journeys; holiday-makers
go on safaris; and others go as missionaries. Africa is considered
a poor, underdeveloped continent, harassed by hunger, and
haunted or stifled by domestic politics. Its future is an enigma.
Not being a businessman or a political person, I can offer only a
personal assessment. One month's visit in Kenya and Uganda
convinced me that human conditions there were pitiable.

How did it happen that my family had the opportunity to
visit Africa?

My wife, Pat, daughter Katina, and I received an invitation
from our church to participate in a missionary journey to Africa.

Letting Go of Baggage

We were full of excitement at such an honor. "What are we supposed to do there?" I asked.

The answer was simple: *You are called to do God's work.*

To attain a clear picture of what a mission to Africa entailed,
we visited Father Alexander Veronis, a dear friend for many years,
pastor of the Greek Orthodox Church in Lancaster, Pennsylvania.
He spoke to us in detail about the mission. He and his wife, Pearl,
devoted their life to missionary work and, at that time, were
deeply involved in helping the indigenous population both
materially and spiritually. He played us a video documenting the
lamentable conditions of the people and then enthusiastically
pointed out missionaries at work in their efforts to alleviate the
hardships. The pictures were heart-breaking showing poverty and
starvation, the emaciated bodies of children, and the deplorable
conditions of infants and parents, barefoot, their clothing in tatters. The video ended by showing a group of American young
adults interacting with village children and bringing joy to their
lives.

The evidence of the desperate plight of the Africans in the
video was depressing. "I have been there several times," Father
Alexander said. "Now, twenty-five young Greek Americans, including my son Luke, are there helping to build homes, schools, and
worship centers. Initially Luke went to Kenya for a month; the one
month turned into six months, which turned into a year. I think
he wants to become a lifelong missionary."

"It's a phenomenal contribution," I said. I could see Pearl
and Father Alexander's emotional involvement.

"It's a drop in the ocean," he said. "We need more workers."
He looked at me with a penetrating eye. "Peter, it's time that you
and your wife and daughter participate. It's an experience of a
lifetime," he said.

Astonished at his boldness, I said, "What do you think we
could contribute?"

"Anything! Those people need any help they can get with
our church ministry. As a therapist, you can help troubled individuals and troubled families. You can teach family-living skills.
Just being there, even for a while, will touch many souls and give
the people a ray of hope."

148

Inspired by exposure to the superior achievements of the young missionaries and the zeal of this priest, I smiled, still feeling unable to respond to such a challenge. A part of me wanted to say, *As a self-employed man, how can I leave my practice and domestic responsibilities and go to Africa as a missionary?* An equally strong part within me wanted to accept unconditionally this challenge. *If I don't do something like this now,* I thought, *when will I be able to do it?* "Father Alexander," I said, "give me a couple of days. I need to think about your request."

That night, I kept waking up. Images of the African situation unfolded vividly in front of me. Swarthy faces with enormous black eyes glowed with genuine yearning for a benevolent hand to touch them; starving kids were glad to receive a warm meal. *Why am I so privileged while others are so deprived?* I saw myself, swimming in comfort—living in my comfortable home, enjoying life in a wealthy country, making a reasonably good living, and having more than enough for our needs. *How can I allow those humans to be deprived of the basics?* The day following the conversation with Father Alexander, my wife and I discussed what we could possibly offer the people in Africa. Pat responded with enthusiasm: "Let's all go as a family. I'm sure we can help as a family." She told Katina about the decision, and both of them felt excited and touched.

Father Jonas, a native African priest, and Father Emmanuel, a Greek American resident missionary, received us at the Kenya airport. Their warm welcome embraced our souls. Along with eight other missionaries, they took us to a simple yet sacred chapel where Byzantine icons, those quick sketches of divinity, underscored thoughts of eternity. The sweet fragrance of incense permeated the air, blending with the smell of flowers that encircled the altar. An *a cappella* choir sang a doxology. Melodious voices full of extraordinary poetry soared with passion straight to the spiritual target, God.

Father Jonas emerged from the altar wearing colorful vestments and holding in his hands the mysteries of heaven, a lit candle. "Everything is dark here in Africa, but the light of Christ shines upon all," he said gently. He held a high station in his land, a pastor and spiritual leader of thousands. He welcomed our group and wished us a pleasant stay. Briefly, he pointed out the conditions and needs of his people. Then, lifting his candle high, he said, "Beloved brothers and sisters, thank you for keeping our candle burning brightly."

We were named the "Teaching Group" and were requested to visit the smaller communities around Nairobi, before moving on to other parts of Kenya and Uganda. There was a uniqueness about the way the native Africans received us. Glowing faces, joyful clapping, drum banging, dancing, singing, bodies swaying back and forth in unison—all this jollification served as a prelude to our program. We asked what their songs meant. Someone who spoke fluent English volunteered explanations. One song spoke of the hardships created by social evils in their homeland, and how the comforting teachings of Christ offered a new way of life. Another song spoke of the generosity of virtuous souls who were eager to alleviate the needs of the poor. Other songs were hymns of praise to a God of love and compassion.

The lyrics, composed mostly by young people, were sung with enthusiasm and served a purpose—to teach a lesson about God, and inspire everyone to live a godly life. As I listened to the interpreter, I felt admiration for the initiative of the leaders of the youth and the receptivity of their followers. They were hardworking people, dedicated to a mission of physical, material, and spiritual survival.

Kenya and Uganda are countries that experience widespread poverty and deprivation. In each region we visited, I witnessed lack of food, drinking water, and clothing, and an absence of medical care and medicine.

In a remote region of West Kenya, I was introduced as Dr. Peter. Within the same hour, I saw a line of women heading in our direction, each carrying infants, and each followed by two or three additional children. I was told that they had brought their children to see me, the doctor. I did not know whether to laugh or cry. The poor innocents heard the word *doctor* and came for help. With regrets, I had to explain that I was not a medical doctor, that in America people who pursue higher education are able to gain the title *doctor*. I watched the crowd retreating, their faces sad with disappointment that I was not a *real* medical doctor.

Higher education? Higher education was nonexistent in the area. Even elementary education was limited, each class containing about eighty students. School conditions were primitive; the buildings were old with tin roofs, large rooms with bare walls, and uncomfortable wooden desks where three or four students sat squeezed together. Yet, each class was peaceful and well-behaved. Katina, then eleven years old, remarked: "You guys are very quiet. In America, there are only sixteen in my class, and you wouldn't believe how much noise we make." She taught African kids American songs, and she showed them how to blow bubbles with gum we had brought from the United States. She served as a nurse distributing Band Aids to the barefoot kids who hurt themselves when working in the fields.

In West Kenya we visited a school of seven hundred students. All of them were barefoot, although it was winter. When it rained, the classes had to pause, for the noise on the tin roofs was deafening. During recess, the students were required to plow the field for half an hour, and then come back to class. For lunch, they were served a dish of corn boiled in milk, and a banana. Following lunch, they invited Katina to join in their games.

Katina was the main attraction one afternoon when she showed the children how to inflate a balloon. We had brought with us several hundred colorful balloons, and we gave one to each student. I will never forget their excitement. It was the first time they had seen a balloon; they thought it was a fantastic gift. I said to Katina, "Close your eyes for a second and imagine you see these kids visiting Toys 'Я' Us!" Katina replied: "Dad, they'd go out of their minds. A simple balloon makes them so happy—they wouldn't know what to do with all those toys."

That particular evening, as the stars studded the dark-blue sky, four boys arrived outside the tent where we were staying; they were prepared to entertain us. Benjamin, a nine-year-old boy, held a homemade violin; it had one string attached to a hollow bamboo stick. The bow consisted of a bent stick whose ends were connected by a string. Paradoxically, this instrument made a sweet sound, as the boys, in full harmony, sang "Twinkle, Twinkle, Little Star." The singing continued in the Swahili language while the boys, with lim-

151

ber body rhythm, danced for us. It was a blessing to watch them and to observe their contented spirit of togetherness.

Next, we visited several regions where people lived a harsh and difficult life, lacking basic needs and comforts that we so easily take for granted. In spite of these hardships, there was love and desire to offer hospitality and to share their faith in Christ. Unlike our church participation in the United States, their worship was full of enthusiasm and energy as they sang, shouted joyfully, clapped, and danced, showing a spirited participation in the services that made God's presence real in their midst.

Three hours from Nairobi, in a village named Nyeri, we found a small convent occupied by five nuns; three were from Finland and two from Greece. Their mission was to take care of forty young children from the surrounding villages. A priest in his late sixties was spiritual director of this convent. He looked like a prophet with his striking bluish eyes, and he had a gracious disposition. Impressed by his dedicated service to these children, I asked how many years he had been a priest. He answered with a beautiful smile: one year.

"One year?"

Noticing my curious look, he said, "I used to be a judge in Athens, Greece. When I retired, I decided to do something worthwhile with what is left in my life. I studied three years for the ministry and became a priest."

"What brought you to Africa?"

"I wanted to erase some of my sins," he said in a contrite voice.

I paused in silence, not knowing what to say. He continued: "I was gifted in the area of words. I was accustomed to use words to manipulate and control others. I thought I could influence others to see things my way. As a judge, I had the power to evaluate people, judge them, and condemn them. I devoured people with words. Arrogantly, I did many wrong things."

Amazed at the sudden confession of a man I had met for the first time in my life, I looked at him with admiration for such an unusual transition. A man holding a prestigious position, a judge in Athens for many years, he abandoned what was probably a luxurious retirement and came to help the indigenous of Africa!

Sitting with him over a modest meal consisting of boiled greens, a few black olives, and a piece of dry bread was a humbling experience. I believed I was in the presence of a holy man. I felt lighter and content. Rarely had I felt so rewarded and so peaceful. What this priest had discovered was a life of simplicity, a service to the less fortunate that gave him inner joy. He said, "I thank God who pointed a new direction for me. Here I don't have to win friends. Here I learned how to love God by caring for the needy. These people genuinely believe that God is the owner and giver of all good things. They are free in spirit, never complain, are content with the little they have, and they know that tomorrow is in God's hands. A simple meal a day, and something simple to wear, makes them happy. I have decided to spend the remainder of my life in this place."

Perhaps the former judge captured, now as a priest, the exuberant spirit of simple caring and sharing. Escaping conformity to the world of affluence, he stood among the indigenous of Africa in all humility and kindness, making himself available as their spiritual father.

In Uganda, we met Theodore Nakiama, an old black bishop, a devout spiritual leader of a very large congregation. His hospitality was simple; he welcomed us with genuine gratitude for our presence, and he told us stories about his work and the needs that he was trying to meet. "Somebody gave us a gift of a thousand dollars," he said and smiled. "I did not know what to do with such an amount. I decided to drill a well. Water is a major issue in this part of the world. Now, many people walk three or four kilometers to the well to fill their containers. They are as happy as can be, pumping water into their plastic buckets. We need to have many more wells drilled, and that's a major expense," he added with an imploring sigh.

When we returned to the United States, Pat and I spoke to several people about Kenya and Uganda's water situation. A few benevolent souls offered help immediately, and within two years, seven more drinking wells were drilled. One wonders how many hundreds of wells could be drilled in that vast land that is blessed with fertile soil and natural beauty.

153

We bonded with many of the African people and promised them help and correspondence. A day before our departure, Father Paul Mavisi approached me and said, "Dr. Kalellis, may I speak with you in private?"

"Of course," I replied.

"I need a big favor from you."

"What can I do for you?" I asked, wondering what that favor could be.

"When you go back to your country, stretch out your arms," he demonstrated the motion. "Give a huge hug of thanks to our American friends. Tell them how grateful we are for their help. Tell them that we love them and shall pray for their good health and prosperity." That was the *big favor* that Father Paul Mavisi requested.

The following September, Katina returned to school. For her English class, she wrote a paper entitled "Never Take Life for Granted." Her remarks included the following:

"When my parents told me that we were going to Africa, I was excited but I did not know what to expect. Was I in shock when we arrived! The room I shared with my parents was damp and cold. We slept on the floor. After a brief visit to Nairobi, we started an eight-hour journey to West Kenya driven in an ambulance along the bumpy roads. We arrived in a school in Gimengwa, and seven hundred kids, aged three to sixteen, welcomed us, singing and banging on big drums. At nights we slept on a hard floor in sleeping bags under mosquito nets. The mosquitoes in Africa are huge and cause malaria. Everything was a big chore, whether it was cooking or washing dishes. The bathroom consisted of an outhouse in the open field. To brush our teeth or get a drink of water, we had to boil the water, filter it, and then boil it again.

"Not many eleven-year-olds have had an experience like mine. Being exposed to life in Africa made me realize that the reason many people in America are unhappy is because the life we live here is so complex. We have too much of everything. In Africa, the people do not know any other way, so they are happy to have what is available to them. We spend time wondering about unimportant decisions such as, should I buy Ivory soap, Dial, or Dove. People in Africa are concerned about where they can find water to drink, and how many kilometers they have to walk barefoot to find a doctor. Going to Africa changed my outlook on life. I am grateful to live in America."

Katina's experience has served her well as she goes through life. Like her, we too feel blessed for having had such a rich experience. We went to Africa as teachers, and we came back as students. We learned a great deal from these people. In their simplicity, there was wisdom, and we gained more than we were able to give. If there was material poverty, it was concealed by the wealth of spiritual joy.

Lessons I Have Learned

- I have learned to be grateful for each day. Every morning I glance out my window and appreciate the wonders of nature—the sky, sun, breeze, trees, flowers—and I say: "This is the day that the Lord has made for you. Be glad and find joy in it." I have learned to greet and welcome each day as a precious gift. I cherish it and try to live it fully and meaningfully.

- It is important for me and all humans to develop an attitude of gratitude. I appreciate and am content with what I have, and with genuine gratitude I thank God for all his blessings. With good choices and some effort on my part, whatever I really need comes my way.

- A lasting lesson came from Father Paul Mavisi when he explained to his people a line from the Lord's Prayer, "Give us this day our daily bread." He suggested that besides food, we need God's grace to sustain our soul and maintain a spirit of gratitude. We may not have much, but we can be grateful for God's love for us.

- "Complaints about what we do not have are fruitless and futile," Father Paul added. "Do not worry about transient things. Think of the animals that surround us. The elephants, the lions, giraffes—all living creatures trust in God for their nourishment. The gnats, the glorious singing of the nightingale, the birds on the branch—all give thanks to God."

- If we suffer a tragedy and have no possessions left, we can reconsider the fact that we are alive. Our life is a miracle, and this is the greatest gift that is ours to cherish. We can be grateful for each breath we take, for each heartbeat. God will never let us down. His plan will unfold gradually, as we make an effort to improve our life.

- Our pains and aches are messengers. We need to listen to them and try to understand their message. Suffering may be a given, but problems provide a choice. Even if arbitrary, the choice ultimately rests upon nothing more than the suffering person's will and ability to say, This is what I'm going to do.

- People with great faith or strong spiritual ties to God tend to be accepting of what happens in their lives, whether it be deprivation of material things, lack of medical care, or the affliction of suffering. They face reality in the best way they can, believing that their current condition is just a temporary state, a preparation for the blessing of the life to come. Those with little or no faith rely more on their own courage to face adversity.

Additional Thoughts

If we are only involved in our individuality and pursue our own needs, we tend to forget that there are other people in this world who lack major necessities for their survival. We have more than we need, and yet we still wonder why we are somewhat unhappy in spite of our wealth and abundance of goods. One of the reasons may be that a full stomach cannot think of a hungry person. Simply, when we become complacent in our daily life, and we ignore the needs of others. They need our help, and we need to help them. You may ask: "What am I supposed to do? Feed the millions who are starving?" No one person can do that. However, if you feed even one person, you will experience the joy that comes from helping someone.

16

The Mystery of Death

Some animals have the capacity to draw out of us the best that we have, and because of their shorter life spans, mark poignant chapters in our own lives.

—Wendell Shackelford

Early in the morning of Tuesday, February 24, 2004, the rising sun peered through the window and shone on my twin girls, who were in an intimate embrace, sleeping. As soon as I began to get out of bed, their eyes blinked, showing a glitter of hunger. Every morning followed a similar pattern: they were at my bedside, waiting for me to wake up and feed them. The realization of what I had to do on this particular Tuesday made my heart palpitate. I looked at them, scratched their heads gently, and felt very sad, knowing that this was the last day of their lives. Our twins, Lucy and Ethel—that's what we had named our cats—were only seven years old. Before the day ended, they would finally be released from their terminally ill conditions.

An hour later, Pat held Ethel in her arms, just as she had held our daughter Katina when she was a baby twenty-three years ago. Katina, teary eyed, drove us to our veterinary clinic to have the two sisters euthanized. Gently, I held my Lucy and kept looking at her gorgeous green eyes. She stared back at me, her eyes expressing curiosity, despair, and fear. Lucy had suffered for two years with failing kidneys, and Ethel was plagued for three years with acute diabetes, for which I gave her two shots of insulin a day. Both cats had been under the vet's care during those years, and eventually they had reached the stage where the prognosis was not good. Empathetically, the vet had told us the time would come when we must do what was within our power to relieve the suffering of our pets.

"As painful as their loss will be to you, euthanizing them will be an act of kindness, an expression of love."

The time had now come. The vet gave both cats a sedative to relax them. Seeing our tears, he reassured us that our cats would feel no pain. He was a gentle man who knew our pets well and had treated them faithfully. As Lucy and Ethel, lying face-to-face, slowly faded away, they turned their eyes upon me with a look of helpless affection expressing their love for us, mingled with supplication—*We really don't want to die.* In that glance was speech more lucid than human words and more moving than our tears. A poetic line, whose origin I could not remember, surfaced in my mind: *In the glance of the speechless animal there is a discourse that only the soul of the wise can really understand.* All three of us stood by them till their last breath; instead of the words we could not utter, thoughts raced through our minds as our souls sought solace.

For days and weeks, I kept thinking about Lucy and Ethel, especially at feeding time. Their peaceful ending left a lasting lesson, even a tinge of envy. They suffered and died, but they did not seem to make a "problem" of it. Domestic animals seem to have few complications in their lives. They eat when they are hungry, sleep when they are tired. Instinct rather than anxiety seems to govern their few preparations for the future.

As far as we can understand, animals are so busy with what they are doing at the moment that it never enters their brain to ask whether life has a meaning or a future. For animals, contentment consists of cherishing life in the immediate present, not in searching for assurance that there is a whole future of joys ahead. Walt Whitman's words in *Leaves of Grass* emphatically summarize the same thought:

> *I think I could turn and live with animals,*
> *they are so placid and self-contained;*
> *I stand and look at them long and long.*

The above lines challenge our perceptions of life and our increasing anxiety about it. We are the only living creatures who are anxious about life because we know that someday we will die. No matter how much we try to understand and accept the reality of death, it seems unbearable that this loved one, this special person, this unique human being in our life, died. On countless occasions we fantasize how we will react when death strikes. Part of us dies when a loved one who has been part of our life is gone forever.

We speak in euphemisms to avoid pain, although we know that our loved one has not *passed on,* nor *departed,* nor *expired,* nor *passed away.* Our loved one has *died.* A loss does not cause simply emotional pain and depressive feelings; it causes actual physical symptoms: dizziness, dry mouth, headaches, loss of appetite, palpitations, and chest tightness. Any one of these is a normal reaction, part of the grieving process, which takes its own time.

For most of us who are beyond the middle years, there is nothing scarier than facing the mystery of our own death. We have no knowledge of what happens after our life ends. Mentally, we say, *The journey of life begins with birth and ends with death.* The time of our death, the last beat of our heart, will always remain unknown to us. We fear death because we really do not know *how* it will come to us individually. We know it takes away everything that we own and call our own, including our body, our hopes, and our dreams. In leaving this world and moving on to an unknown destiny, we take nothing with us.

As we gradually mature, we are able to accept the reality that our earthly life will come to an end some day. We have had our share of fantasies, successes, and failures, and conceivably we can still have more of these. Yet, it is time for serious thinking. When we notice our physical changes, we can turn inward and realize the unchangeability of our soul. It is a time when we can become spiritually radiant as we begin to think that our end is not yet in sight. *Spiritual* aging can enrich our life with meaning and purpose; at the same time, we still take care of our physical vitality and social responsibilities. It is an opportunity for each one of us to ask ourselves: *How can I live well until I die? How can I prepare myself to view my death with peace, patience, acceptance, and fearless-*

*ness? How can I prepare myself so that death will not come to me or my
relatives as a shock?* These questions may be difficult to answer. Yet,
this is our challenge and we need to provide an answer.

Periodically I think of an old Greek song that makes me smile:

Should death knock at your door,
Welcome him, not as an intruder.
Sit him on your right side and offer him wine,
Have no fear of the Grim Reaper, his visit is divine.

When death comes to a loved one, we reexamine our life. We
become acutely aware that our turn may be next. We review our
past wrongs, our unwitting errors, and our failures, whether real
or imagined, in order to rectify them. Thus, self-recrimination
becomes a way to undo possibly all the events that make us feel
guilty. As we recall the words we have said that we should not have
said, or actions we have taken that we should not have taken, we
understand our guilt. Yet, we also need to stop and ask ourselves:
Whoever went through this life without some failure? Although most
of us believe in a loving and forgiving God, we have difficulty in
letting go of our past and realizing our human vulnerability. Guilt
tends to make our lives miserable and passive; we keep telling
ourselves: If only I had treated the one I loved more kindly—
understood the full extent of the illness—called a doctor
sooner—expressed my affection frequently—had been more
available...

These "if only" residues of guilt are a covert self-
punishment, and they delay healing. We would feel better if we
remembered or recounted sweet memories, pleasant experiences, meaningful dialogues, and intimate times that we spent
with the beloved person.

On the Thursday following our final farewell to our cats,
dejected as I was, I went to my office for my 10:00 a.m. appoint-
ment with a client. We will call her Eve and her daughter Anne.
Eve looked sad, and as soon as she saw me, she burst into tears.

"My best friend's only daughter was killed in a car accident
on the Garden State Parkway last night," she said. "My daughter
was in the car with her. Anne has only minor bruises; she's okay

161

but feels terribly depressed. The other girl graduated from college only a few months ago. She and Anne grew up together, and her mother and I have been friends since elementary school. Oh, Dr. Kalellis, it's not fair!"

"Your daughter was lucky. I'm sorry about the tragic accident. Death is never fair. A car accident, a heart attack—any form of sudden death reminds us of the fact that we are fragile. We have no other choice but to realize the limitations of our physical existence and to be careful to protect our life."

"I want to be of some comfort to my friend, but I do not know what to say."

"Regardless of what anyone says to or does for a grieving person, when death strikes, there is no instant comfort. Think of your friend. She has lost her daughter, the child of her dreams. Now, besides her feelings, she has to face the painful reality that her daughter is no longer present. She senses the emptiness in her home. Other people's similar losses are of no consequence to her. For a few seconds she may be sympathetic, but she is struggling with her own emotions."

"What do you think I could do?"

"Your actual presence in this most difficult time will provide some relief. Just be there," I said. "You don't need to say much or to sound brave. In the days to come, visit your friend often. Bring her a cooked meal. That provides practical comfort as well as nourishment. A friend's benevolent presence means a great deal of comfort."

"What can friends do for a grieving person?"

"Initially, after we offer the bereaved our condolences, we sit and listen. Grieving people have a lot to say about their loss. We can listen with empathy and be attentive to stories they tell about their loved one. We should not say, "I understand," because in reality we do not understand. It is better to say, "I know you are hurting," or "It is hard to bear such pain"—and pause for a couple of minutes as you keep eye contact. Our silence gives the person a chance to verbalize his or her feelings, and this tends to be therapeutic."

"My mother is now ninety-three years old, and I know that some day she will die," said Eve. "When the thought crosses my mind, I dread thinking about it, although I know she had a full life." She sighed. "I guess I want her to live forever."

"One day we will all be gone. The loss of a mother, regardless of age, is a major loss, and you are going to feel it. Even if she lives to be a hundred and ten or more, it will not alleviate the pain when the inevitable occurs; it will leave emptiness and sadness. Your good memories about her and your life together will provide some relief."

"Death of young people is particularly sad, isn't it?" said Eve.

"Death plays no favorites. He is truly impartial, and sooner or later he will pay each of us a visit. Death of young or old through accidents, cancer, tumors of the brain, and diseases of all sorts is just another aspect of life's realities. But a person in pain, such pain as caused by the loss of a loved one, cannot think rationally. Logic cannot possibly give us—or them—a total understanding of death. It needs to be supported by faith in an unquestionable fact: Death ends our physical presence, but our life continues in a different form, in a different world, in the presence of God, which no logic can comprehend. We derive comfort from knowing that people we love do not die; they are physically absent, and yet they are forever present in our hearts."

Silently, Eve studied my face. "Do you ever think of death?"

"Of course! Every day. Especially when I am physically ill or have unusually strange symptoms in my body. I say to myself: *What if this is it? Could this be my time to go?* At the same time, I come up with the answer: *Peter, stop playing God. When your time comes, there is nothing you or anybody can do about it. It will be your time to go.*

"Another of life's mysteries is the time of our death. How, when, and under what conditions will we die? Our last breath and the last beat of our heart will always remain unknown. No human knows the day or the hour or the way of departure from this life. Most people are terrified as they ponder upon that mysterious moment when the soul departs from the body to return to its Creator.

"In the depth of our souls," I continued, "among the crevices of our desires and hopes, lingers the fear of death. Our fear of death may be a subconscious excitement over the life beyond. It is the

163

hesitation of a baby taking its initial steps. Our fear of death, like the baby's hesitation, initiates our first steps toward immortality. Understandably, all of us fear the unknown, life after death. Here is a thought: If God created a beautiful world for our physical existence and happiness, would he not prepare a place for our souls?"

"Has anything been said or written about what happens at the moment of death?"

"Stories about dying experiences have been written, but does anyone actually know what happens at the precise moment? In death, the soul separates from the body, as the butterfly frees itself from its own cocoon and returns to its Creator. The Good Book claims: "…Unless a grain of wheat falls into the earth and dies, it remains just a single grain; but if it dies, it bears much fruit" (John 12:24). There is another comforting thought in Psalm 23: Even though I walk through the darkest valley, I fear no evil; for you are with me; your rod and your staff—they comfort me….Surely goodness and mercy shall follow me all the days of my life, and I shall dwell in the house of the LORD my whole life long" (v. 4, 6).

"All of that implies that you have faith," Eve said.

"Without faith, life is not easy, and death becomes fearsome."

With a glitter of relief in her eyes, she added in a lower tone, "Birth and death are two ends of the same yardstick, life."

"True! In the Bible, the Book of Ecclesiastes confirms it: "For everything there is a season, and a time for every matter under heaven: a time to be born, and a time to die" (Eccl 3:1–2).

"In truth, everything that is born dies. That is a reality, although a difficult one to accept, Eve said. "Intellectually I understand all that, and I know that some day *I* will die. I just hope that I don't become a burden to my family or suffer a prolonged and painful illness. Most of the time, I'm not afraid of death. I have lived a fulfilled life thus far, and God has been good to me. I have no regrets, I'm happy."

"Eve, I'm glad you feel that way. I'm closer to the end of my earthly journey than you are. I'm focusing on accepting the reality of my demise. Once I accept it, then I can enjoy the rest of my life to its fullest. I want a peaceful ending; I have no guarantee of that. Day by day I'm getting closer to my death.

"It is good to remind ourselves from time to time that our days on this planet are numbered. The journey of life, which begins with birth, eventually comes to an end. It's healthy to reflect on this thought in a positive way. Death is an inescapable fact of life. Personally, I feel at peace when I leave it in the hands of our Creator. He is the author of life and death. Worrying about my end will not lengthen my years, not even by one day."

She smiled. "I wonder how I will feel when I sense that death is near."

"I cannot say with confidence how anyone feels, but I can tell you what I believe: Death separates us from our loved ones— a sad reality. It leaves behind no power or control that we can use over life or people. We cannot take anything with us; we leave behind all we have accumulated—our money, material possessions, homes, properties, wealth. Simply, we need to remind ourselves that the earth is the Lord's, and everything upon the earth belongs to him."

"I don't have many possessions," Eve said. "We have one daughter; we live in a small house; my husband and I have good jobs. We are content. I wonder what multimillionaires think about all this." I can't imagine what death must mean to those who have many possessions, who have nothing to worry about, and enjoy luxury and prosperity in everything.

"Nobody knows. Some people live in their own world of illusions. Personally, I do not envy those with material accumulations, wealth, and status symbols. I do envy people who are especially gifted in the arts: painting, sculpting, theater, poetry, and creative writing. Their artistic contributions speak of the Master Artist, God, who is the giver of all talents. These people have wealth in their talents; a legacy that transcends their own death. But to the person who is destitute and hungry, homeless, worn down by age, afflicted by a horrible and painful disease, the thought of death may be comforting."

"Doctor, what makes me sad is knowing that I will probably leave behind my daughter, and when she is married and has a family, I will not be around to enjoy my grandchildren."

"It is a sad thought. You are a young woman, and you should think of the way that our Creator designed life. Can you imagine the pain you would endure if your child or grandchild should die before you? It is the ultimate pain for parents when their child or grandchild dies—and not such an unusual situation, as your friend tragically discovered.

"The death of family members—especially the loss of children or dear pets—has the greatest impact on us," I continued. "One day we see them, talk to them, touch them, love them genuinely, and suddenly they are no longer around. They leave a void in our heart; we feel sad—which brings us to the realization that we *also* are walking gradually toward the sunset of life. Do I like the thought? No. Nobody does. We can, however, still be loving and lovable till then."

"But sometimes the more we love, the more vulnerable we become."

"True! You can understand why some people resist love. Maybe they are afraid that they will get hurt: "The more I love someone, the more I can get hurt." That can happen. Some people do not want to hear about death, and they protect their feelings by avoiding a loving relationship. Without love, there is so much less to lose. Fear of death keeps us apart from reality, keeps us anxious and isolated emotionally. If I don't share my fear, although I know that others may have similar concerns about dying, then I can avoid such a gruesome subject."

"It's a good point," Eve said. She thought for a brief moment, and in a sad voice, added, "This was not an easy topic to discuss today. I still need more understanding. How can I put death into reasonable perspective in my mind so I can move on with life and living?"

"By the time we meet again next week, you may come up with the answer."

Lessons I Have Learned

- Death has always been a mystery to humans. Death is not always a tragic event, nor is it necessarily beautiful. The death of a young person is truly most painful for the parents and intimate adults. We can comfort them by our presence and a sympathetic attitude.

- The thought of death is frightening to most of us, and yet living with the knowledge that we will die is not nearly as terrifying as the thought of living forever. How could anyone in this world endure a life that went on and on without end?

- I accept death as a part of life, just as I expect sunrise every morning and sunset every evening. Taking a different attitude toward death will help us not to be afraid: learning to think of death not as a dreaded intruder, not as an uninvited guest who interrupts our present life, but as a messenger who takes us to eternal life.

- Think, believe, and trust the Giver of Life. We should place our thoughts in a calmer and healthier perspective in harmony with God's will. Faith in a God of love and compassion helps us to cope with a loved one's death without inflicting unnecessary fear in our heart about our own death.

- My physical body has been the dwelling place of my soul for many years. I am aware that my body is getting old and will ultimately die. My soul will continue its life in the presence of God. What God will do with me after my earthly life is his business. My concern needs to be how I deal with my life while I am still alive.

- Regardless of how old we are, from this moment on we can get excited about what is left of our life, making each day meaningful for ourselves and the people around us. Then we will feel empowered to do whatever needs to be done, to improve the conditions of our life, and to make our society more humane and just.

- Along with our intellectual capacity to understand death, we need to comprehend the impermanent nature of life. Inevitably we will leave behind loved ones, unfulfilled dreams, and unfinished business. Separating from all earthly attachments causes anxiety, anger, and fear. Such is the case of any transition we make when we leave the familiar for the unfamiliar.

Additional Thoughts

Fear, whether instinctual or emotional, is a reality of life. We combat fears according to how we perceive life. Good logic and rational thinking can truly provide solutions to different types of fear. But the fear of death, which young and old experience to some degree, can only be faced by faith in the loving God who created us and continues to give us life. The Christian faith claims that Christ defeated death by his death. His resurrection promises new life. As our earthly life comes to an end, it leaves us with that promise. Logic alone cannot visualize fulfillment of such a promise. Faith is able to see what seems invisible to the eye or incomprehensible to the mind. Yet even the mind may wonder: Would a loving God allow such a tragic end to human life? If a tiny creature of God's creation, such as a beautiful butterfly, can emerge from the cocoon of a dead worm, would it not be possible for God to give us a new body after our death? Logic may have its doubts. But faith says, What seems impossible to the human mind, is possible to God. It is then that our new life will continue in the presence of God.

17

Enjoying the Fruits

Nurturing the self is a lot like tending a garden. In essence the growth of plants is a natural process determined by a variety of forces that are beyond the gardener's control. However, there are some activities on the part of the gardener which are crucial for growth. —Orlo Strunk, Jr.

I designated the day before my seventy-seventh birthday as a day of rest from my usual routine. After swimming for a mile at the YMCA, I decided to work in my garden and get some fresh air. It was a perfect June day—warm weather and not a cloud in the sky. I pulled up the crabgrass and weeds, and when I had finished fertilizing the tomato, zucchini, and cucumber plants, I stood and observed with wonderment their growth. Pat had planted the tiny seeds in February and had tended them indoors during the cold weather. Slowly, thread-thin shoots bearing minute, tender leaves surfaced from small starter cells of soil. Under Pat's diligent care, sunning and watering them, they grew gradually until they were ready for transplanting into our garden. Now we had clusters of green tomatoes. In another six weeks they would be red and ripe. *Such is the mystery of growth,* I thought. *Different seeds developing under the same soil become plants with their own qualities. Who makes these plants grow? Who makes us grow?*

Our human life resembles a garden. It requires diligence, care, nurture, patience, and the removal of obstacles. And just as plants are pruned back to encourage better growth, human life must be "pruned" of bad habits to enable fuller growth of the soul.

"Daddy!" My daughter Katina interrupted my thoughts and asked me to come indoors. "You look so tired," she said. "Gardening is hard work. Come. I've prepared a bubble bath for you. It's ready."

"A bubble bath?" I laughed. "Why a bubble bath?"

"You'll love it. Come now before the water gets cold." She grabbed my hand and led me into the bathroom. Eagerly she untied and removed my shoes.

"Thanks, Sweet Love," I said. "Let me do this myself."

"No, I want to help you," she insisted. I gently pushed her out of the bathroom. With a "daddy's little girl" charm, she said, "Get under the bubbles quickly. Dinner will be ready by the time you come out."

My thoughts wandered back a few years to the time when Katina, a tiny little creature, came into our life and changed our world forever. Pat and I loved her, nurtured her, and created a warm environment for her, enabling her to grow happy and healthy. Today she is a young, reliable, loving, and caring woman. She is a happy person and does beautiful things spontaneously. She loves to cook gourmet meals, and today she prepared a special treat for me: dinner and a bubble bath. *Thank you, Katina.* Remembering her excitement as she'd led me to my bath, I whispered to myself, *What happiness it is to be in love.* A few months ago, on her twenty-fifth birthday, she became engaged to the man of her dreams—a man whose name also happens to be Peter—and she was the happiest I have ever seen her. Pat and I felt rewarded seeing Katina and her Peter happy as they interacted with each other. At the time, she still lived at home, and I appreciated her presence in our life. I knew some day she would leave us and move on to make her own home. My prayer was that the young man she has chosen to marry will appreciate and love her as much as Pat and I do.

Vita Bath inundated the bathroom with a sweet fragrance, and my aging body was scarcely visible in the steamed-up mirror. The water was rather hot, and I practically submerged myself. Soothed, relaxed, and hungry, I kept thinking of dinner.

There was a gentle knock at the door. "Service!" shouted Katina. "Hope you're under the bubbles!"

"I am in heaven. Come in," I said.

Carefully, she brought in a covered tray and placed it near the bathtub. "Dad, stay where you are!"

"What have you got in there? It smells delicious." I turned my head to peek.

"Sizzling meatballs, green olives, small pieces of feta cheese, bread sticks, and a glass of *ouzo* in ice cubes."

I grabbed a meatball; it was soft, tender, hot, and tasty.

"Mommy is setting the table now. Dinner is almost ready." She handed me the glass of ouzo and waved her hand goodbye, saying, "Drink it slowly, and enjoy the meze," the Greek name for hors d'oeuvres.

I took a sip of ouzo, savored it in my mouth, allowing it to trickle down my throat and soothe my stomach. I stretched back in the warm water, munching on a garlic-olive and enjoying another sip of what was served with my daughter's love. I succumbed to a reverie. Still holding my glass, I closed my eyes, reveling in this unprecedented ecstasy. Another glimpse of God's kingdom! Soon, on my mind's screen, appeared a familiar figure, a skinny boy of eight, lighting a candle in front of the icon of Christ in St. Basil's Church in Moria. I blinked, and the skinny boy reappeared, older and taller. This time he was sitting in Alexis' tavern having his first ouzo. How fast the mind travels! In a flash, my early life on the island of Lesvos in Greece paraded in front of my eyes. Pleasantly, I emerged from the dream zone with a grateful smile.

The bubble bath had soothed my tired limbs. My body under the fragrant bubbles became totally relaxed. My mind recalled more events that had occurred in my life from way back. Each event, which flashed through my head, burst forth and disappeared just like a soap bubble. Vivid images of yesterdays went by faster than a weaver's shuttle! *What a metaphor of life*, I thought. Life's dreams and ambitions; the value of achievements; possession of riches, money and glory; fame and influence, fortunes and fantasies, successes and failures, major and minor events—all are temporal. Like soap bubbles, they inflate, glitter for a while, fade, and quickly disappear.

A transition in my life had taken place every seven years; the memory provides quick sketches and scenes of a turbulent child-

171

hood, young adult insecurities, new life in America—the promised land with its infinite possibilities, the seminary, married life and priesthood, middle-year crises and major changes, and the successful move into the field of psychology. I did not always have the courage to face the challenges of life, but I did have the will to overcome obstacles. Something strange within me fueled my confidence to move on. It was not a matter of personal ingenuity or intellectual ability. It was not mere luck or manipulation of circumstances or people. It was rather the miracle-working power that, two thousand years ago, Jesus made known to us, the gift of the Holy Spirit within each human being. It is the divine part, God's power within, that helps us attain our potential as his creation. The once-upon-a-time olive picker in a small Greek village returned to his place of birth, Philadelphia. Today, my arrival in the promised land takes on a deeper meaning. Obviously, there is a great splendor within us, but it can only be unfolded through faith in God, an awareness of his presence in our life, prayer, discipline, hard work, self-acceptance, and self-realization. There is no short cut to the power within.

—᠊᠊᠊᠊᠊᠊᠊᠊᠊᠊᠊᠊᠊

There was another tap at the bathroom door, and a sweet voice interrupted my contemplation.

"Dad, dinner will be served in five minutes. Hurry!"

I had moved from temporal to spiritual and lasting reality, the joy of love. Now I let go of the concept and of the contemplation on vanity and prepared myself for dinner. It was time for a serious transition! Part of having a physical body is the requirement to cherish, within reason, what is available in a physical world. I could not overlook the nonphysical realities of life: faith, hope, and love, three things that are everlasting. I also had to redefine the reality of love, respect, and sensitivity that were available here and now in my own home.

Graciously, Pat sat next to me. My younger daughter, Katina, and her fiancé sat happily among my older children, their spouses, and my grandchildren. My immediate family was present, except for my younger son who lives with his wife in Florida. It was a unique moment to sit in the dining area and see all the happy faces. *My children.* Overwhelmed with joy, I offered grace, grateful to God for his endless blessings, and thanked Pat and all present who had made this day a very special one for me.

The dining table, decorated with flowers and candles, looked elegant. The appetizers and the meal were delicious. "As always, a great dinner," I said. I kept glancing at the radiant faces of my wife and children, faces reflecting a benevolent gaze of joy, and I felt grateful. My presence was appreciated, my comments were listened to, stories that I had told them many times before were accepted with interest as if they were new, points of disagreement were treated with indulgence, and my needs were met caringly. What other blessing besides good health could I ask from God?

As I evaluate the journey of my life, I often wonder what effect my presence and behavior has had on my immediate others—spouse, four children, and friends. Was I accepted and understood without being judged? Was I regarded with affection and respect? Of course I was; otherwise, I would have felt emotionally abandoned. In their presence, I felt genuine love, for they created a nurturing environment in which I was able to mature, to be reflective, to respond to them, and to make my life's transitions responsibly. Over a period of dealing with issues in my personal therapy, and now practicing therapy professionally, I felt fulfilled without knowing how and why. One answer that I can give with certainty is that I have become a better person, more able to care and to love.

I gradually came to the realization that adversities, conflicts, and suffering in our lives do not disappear without a change in what one is and how one lives, thinks, feels, and responds. Human personality is a complex balance of many conflicting claims, forces, tensions, compunctions, and distractions in which an individual manages to be a functioning entity. Changes may occur when there is a desire to change attitude and behavior.

Since we are what we do—not in the career sense, of course, but in our every action—if we want to change what we *are*, we must begin by changing what we *do*; we must undertake a *new* mode of action. The new mode will at first be experienced as difficult, anxiety-provoking, forced, unpleasant, and unnatural.

Remaining in the familiar state of being does not require any effort. It is predictable. To make a change takes responsibility, the ability to respond, an awareness of what may currently be going on, a willingness to take risks, a leap of faith, a concerted effort of will, time, and perseverance.

Years ago, Pat and I both wanted to remodel our house. Neither of us had any idea how involved this undertaking would be. She had envisioned what it would be like, and yet we had to delegate an architect to draw the plans. In time, we had perfect blueprints, including all details to match our preferences. Pat already had a clear picture in her mind how the remodeled house would look once completed, and she was excited.

The blueprints alone were not enough. We had to hire a good contractor to supervise the construction, purchase the needed materials, and employ skillful hands to remodel our house. We are satisfied with the results, and we are still enjoying the newness of our home immensely.

In the process of building or remodeling the house of our life, we may delegate nothing, for the task can be initially accomplished only in the workshop of our mind and heart. When we decide to change—for example, say, *I want to be...*, with a sense of becoming what we were not until now—we may grope toward this vision in the dark, with no guide, no map, and no guarantee. We act as an authority, author, creator, designer, and subject. The total responsibility lies within us, originates with us, and remains with us to the end. It may be of essence to have someone qualified to help us. Yet, it will be no less ours if we enlist the aid of a therapist or a wise mentor. Either of these can guide and direct, offer insights and options, but the effort to bring about a change in our life remains with us. There is no shortcut, no safe-conduct, no easier way. Ultimately, each of *us* makes things happen. We become the architects; we create or re-create our own life.

In written history, we discover people who made a miraculous turnaround. Saul of Tarsus was a fanatic persecutor of the Christian faith. On the road to Damascus, he had an experience that changed him into a fervent follower of Christ and the greatest exponent of Christianity. Faith inspired sinners to become saints, criminals to become noble citizens, and thieves to become honest men. In our times, derelicts, neurotics, substance abusers, and addicts make extraordinary turnabouts and adjust to life's difficulties because of their decision to seek a healthier direction.

It is frustrating to see individuals who are perpetually depressed yet are unwilling to help themselves in their condition.

"I was born depressed, and I have been depressed all my life. I have tried everything and don't know what else I can do," a client once complained to me.

"Your suffering is real to you," I said. "What are you willing to do about it?"

Being depressed or unhappy is a familiar condition that haunts many people, and it can last a long time unless action takes place. It is a predictable state of being if nothing is done about it. However, if the suffering person stays in therapy long enough to examine the symptoms of fear, dependence, and lack of fulfillment, the sufferer may learn that blaming others, circumstances, events, or past traumas are only excuses used for ulterior purposes—perhaps to cover up feelings of fear to reach out, or a sense of inadequacy and personal insecurity. Avoiding the awareness of what the real issues are, the person avoids responsible action to do what needs to be done.

Granted, suffering is sometimes obscure. Anxiety, boredom, dissatisfaction with life, feelings of emptiness, isolation—in all these states of mind, it is hard to see the correlation among thoughts, inner feelings, and the way we live. Yet, no such feelings can be independent of behavior. If the connection among behavior, thought process, and feeling is discovered and understood, we will see how a change in the way we think and live will make for a change in what we feel.

It took time, years of personal therapy and then my own psychological training, to be able to understand and harmonize my thoughts with my feelings. This effort worked for me, and I would recommend it to any person who seeks a better and healthier life.

In spite of the many transitions in my life, these harvest years are an abundant blessing. The yesterdays, good and bad, happy and sad, are gone forever. I am dealing only with the present. During the day, I phone my wife to see how she is, and I inform her what time I will be at home. Just before leaving my office, I call again to say, I am on my way home. As I enter the door, I call, "Love, I'm here!"

We connect. I take a look at her; I treasure her presence and feel lucky. I am a happy man. In my heart, I know that I love her more than any other human being; I know she loves me, and we want our life together to continue for many more years.

Lessons I Have Learned

- Life is like a garden; it can be beautiful and productive. If anything is to grow in it, we need to roll up our sleeves, cultivate the soil, remove crabgrass and weeds, and fertilize the flowers and vegetables. Whatever the obstacles in our life, one by one, we must overcome them.

- It is *our* responsibility to make needed changes. Transitions, which at one time made sense to us, may have been emotionally costly, and healing of emotions was necessary. Respond to each transition with care, and be aware that any new direction requires both planning and responsible action.

- Preoccupation with problems makes us prisoners and controls our life. Make an effort to visualize and to pursue possible solutions. What may have been a good choice at one time may turn out to be a lingering problem. We may have to make a new choice. Any movement for a positive change helps to diffuse our anxiety.

- Adversities are part of life. Obstacles are always present, especially when we are trying to do something different or new. Anger, frustration, negativity, trouble at work or at home can be stifling to growth. Our part is to face adversity with faith and courage, confront the opposing forces, and move on carefully with hope.

- When you find yourself under unusual stress or come to an impasse, do not take your frustration out on others or on those who are close to you. At worst, let them know that your "bad mood" has nothing to do with them, or tell them the specific cause of your current feelings.

- Acceptance of life as it is, and what we do about it or how we adjust to it, is a major step toward maturity. We can fight it or run away from it; but life is what it is, and we cannot always get things our way. Our choice is to take responsible action and change the conditions of our life, without taking advantage of anyone.

- Faith in God's presence in our life is the firmest vehicle to carry us safely on the journey through life. My faith increased as I experienced it and watched it move in the lives of others. Our parents caused our birth, but God gave us and continues to give us the gift of life. Caring and properly providing for our own life will enable it to evolve wisely.

Epilogue

    This book would be incomplete were I not to add a few words of appreciation to my readers. Truly, I feel grateful to all for traveling with me on this adventurous journey through my life. It is my hope that you have extracted something useful from my experiences and lessons.

    I assume that you have identified, in your own life, experiences similar to mine, aspects that parallel mine. It is my hope that I have provided a sense of relief that makes us all people on a similar journey. So, in sharing my life with you, I now dedicate this book to you, to my family and my friends who have enriched my journey.

    I believe in the axiom that humans learn from each other; my intention was simply to convey a message, not to preach. I shared sensitive areas of my life, not to solicit pity, but to share aspects that pave the path toward healing for others who hurt. Our tormented minds need help and healing; these are available to us as we look compassionately into the reality of other people's lives.

    The world in which we live is complex and conflicting, making our daily life a mystery. Rhythms are all around us: the beat of our hearts, the pulse of our blood, and the change of tides and seasons that leave us in awe. There is a harmony in nature that raises the perennial question: *Why can we not maintain harmony in our own homes and peace among people and nations?*

    How many attempts have you made to understand the world around you—the family and the society in which you live? How many attempts have you made to discover a magic formula, an effective prescription to protect yourself from the adversities and absurdities of life? What did you find? Perhaps you found friendly advice or a suggestion from a wise person, or a reading that helped you rediscover the potential for a better life—all these may have brought you further toward inner contentment.

The variety of themes this book offers came from the depth of my heart. Gleanings from my studies and experiences of people who sought my services were most helpful. All this, interwoven with events and personal experiences, taught me many lessons. It would take a volume to encompass all the lessons. Instead, I have ended each chapter with "Lessons I Have Learned," which, in essence, carry the theme of each chapter. The aim is to instill in my readers faith and self-confidence, a capacity to look toward the future with courage and optimism, and with excitement over the thought that, while we have no control about life in general, we can take charge of our own life. It is hard work and an ongoing struggle to maintain a reasonably good life for ourselves while preserving our personal integrity. That life is a struggle is not an exaggeration. It *is* a struggle, and yet it leads to a rediscovery of our potential and joy inherent in our humanity.

Through the journey of my life and its challenges, I have tried to recount experiences and bittersweet events that taught me a unique lesson: *Good things are only accomplished through hard work, patience, persistence, and prayer.* Even small, insignificant episodes in the course of my development gave me character and shape. In spite of the obstacles, I embraced life without extravagant expectations but with gratitude for what I was able to learn through my own efforts and the assistance of others. I was and continue to be satisfied with the rewards. Consciously, I erased any tinge of jealousy that crossed my mind—jealousy over what others possessed and I did not. I am able to admire the accomplishments of others, and I congratulate them for their achievements.

I believe that every human being can take a chunk of the big rock called life and carve a piece to his or her own liking. Most of us are the architects of our own lives. As such, we have a choice to make plans; otherwise, others will plan our life. Of course, at times we become confused, and life seems dark and chaotic. We have no direction, no purpose, no goal in sight. Currents and crosscurrents rise and threaten our existence. When we have no answer, we become scared and we agonize. This sort of emotional condition causes fatigue and passivity, resulting in frustration and even anger at ourselves and at the world around us. A negative reaction to accept what is real and important in our life will waste precious energy trying to change the world around us. We can make the changes we need to redesign our personal life so our journey may continue creatively and rewardingly. Out of this personal effort, we can help our world become a better place to live.

. We are told by some psychologists that the first half of life is spent in struggling with the problems of status and survival. We must get an education. We must earn a living. We must learn to relate to others in ways that contribute to our survival. We become preoccupied with these goals. At times, coping mechanisms may sap all our energies, and we actually begin to believe that *this* is life, *this* is all there is. Life is coping, scratching for a living, struggling to make ends meet, groaning for a secure place in the sun, doing a job. This means that life is one great problem, and that we are essentially, and only, problem-solvers.

You and I have another side, and that other side will itself be known sooner or later. In a sense, this other side says, *Look, there is more to life than solving problems and achieving goals. There is a quality to life, and I want you to meet it. Let go of the baggage and enjoy the journey!* Hopefully, this *voice* that came to me in recollecting aspects of my life may also come to you. Be alert. *Seek quality, but strive more for significance and less for success.* Regardless of your age or status, coming to realize who you really are in all your complexity, even at the eleventh hour, can provide the unexpected miracle in your life. Look out for this miracle and embrace it.